D0242059

THE CHALLENGE OF ARCHERY

DON STAMP

The Challenge
of
ARCHERY

ADAM & CHARLES BLACK
LONDON

FIRST PUBLISHED 1971
SECOND EDITION 1979
BY A. AND C. BLACK (PUBLISHERS) LIMITED
35 BEDFORD ROW, LONDON WC1R 4JH

©1971 DON STAMP

ISBN 0 7136 1260 6

DEDICATION

To My Wife

PRINTED BY J. W. ARROWSMITH LTD.
WINTERSTOKE ROAD, BRISTOL 3

Contents

	FOREWORD	9
1.	THE CHALLENGE OF ARCHERY	11
2.	TAKING IT UP	15
3.	SAFETY AND ETIQUETTE	25
4.	LEARNING TO SHOOT: TARGET	31
5.	LEARNING TO SHOOT: FIELD AND CLOUT	43
6.	CHOOSING YOUR OWN EQUIPMENT	55
7.	IMPROVING YOUR SHOOTING	74
8.	COMPETITIVE ARCHERY	91
9.	VARIETY IN ARCHERY	99
10.	ARCHERY FOR THE HANDICAPPED	112
11.	JUNIOR ARCHERY	117
12.	CARE, MAKING AND MAINTENANCE	124
13.	THE ORGANISATION OF ARCHERY	138
	SELECTED READING	145
	GLOSSARY OF TERMS	146
	INDEX	153

Illustrations

Photographs

1. Bracing the bow 32
2. Setting the sight for initial practice 32
3. Establishing the standing position 33
4. Fingers on the string 35
5. The Preparation Position 35
6. Full Draw 37
7. The Loose 40
8. Full Draw. Field Style 46
9. Aiming at the Clout (1) 52
10. Aiming at the Clout (2) 53
11. First World Field Championship 103
12. Use of flight bow 105
13. Clout shooting 107
14. Popinjay Mast 109
14a. Popinjay Technique 109
15. Ada Nightingale of Crowthorne Archers 113

Acknowledgements

The author wishes to thank the following photographers for permission to reproduce certain photographs:
Plate 11 B. Bengtson, *Plate 12* W. A. Sillince, *Plate 14* K. Skipper,

Drawings

1. A simple bow 18
2. A safe length of arrow 22
3. Three sights 60
4. Shorter range sights 61
5. The Archer's Paradox 64
6. Two Shafts 65
7. One Shaft 66
8. Types of Pile 67
9. Two Nocks 67
10. The Draw-force line 81

11.	E.S.A.R.	83
12.	Trajectory	107
13.	The string jig	126
14.	Fletching Angles	129
15.	Feather Burner	130
16.	Bracer and Tab	131
17.	The Quiver	133
18.	Boxed Butt	135
19.	The Target Stand	136

Foreword

The late 'Bill' Dixon as National Coaching Organiser had long deplored the absence of a book on Archery which coaches could unhesitatingly recommend to enquirers, beginners and the more experienced alike. I was the more pleased, therefore, when he asked me to read through the first chapter of a book he himself had undertaken to write. Unfortunately he died before he could make further progress with the work.

Even so, readers will be able to benefit from his clear exposition of the Basic Method of Target Archery in Chap. 4 which I am proud to include in this work as a tribute to a friend and deeply respected colleague in Archery Coaching for many years. As for the rest of the book – the responsibility and opinions are mine, but I hope it will at least go some way to offer the information that Bill himself might otherwise have supplied.

Here, too, I would like to acknowledge the help given me by Don Morland in preparing for publication the photographs illustrating basic technique, to Jon Toll for posing for the shots, to Carol Dixon for her help and encouragement, and to my wife for her patience in hearing all this read over many, many times.

Don Stamp.

Chapter 1

The Challenge of Archery

What is the challenge, you may ask? Is not archery just a game, a recreation, a somewhat antiquated revival of one of man's oldest occupations no longer of value in sustaining life and limb? Well, I'll try to explain how it is that archery has offered me and so many others a permanent challenge, an inexhaustible fascination and – in all seriousness – a way of life.

Essentially archery may seem simple. You get a bow that is within your strength, nock an arrow that is long enough, draw back the string, adjust for aim and let the shaft fly. It sounds too easy, but it is this very simplicity that increases the difficulty. The minutest variation in technique, the least doubt and uncertainty, and errors begin to creep in, causing despondency, anxiety and frustration until the cause is pin-pointed and rectified. Yet when all goes well and the technique is right, the archer looses the shaft with calm confidence and knows with absolute certainty from the moment of loose that it will find its intended mark. Even poor archers have these moments of controlled certainty and ensuing satisfaction – better archers have them more often, that's the difference. Good instruction and constant attention to detail will ensure that you reduce the 'bad' shots to a minimum with the object of eliminating them altogether. Yet it is the ever-present possibility of failure to reach perfection that makes archery worth while. If one could be sure of always hitting the mark aimed at there would be no challenge, no sense of achievement, and no pleasure, except in bow-hunting where the challenge would then relate less to the archery than to the stalk and the risk of personal danger.

In physical terms the archer's effort is not negligible. After a day-long target competition in which 150 arrows may be loosed, or a field shoot where miles of rough hilly country may be traversed while shooting 112 arrows, the archer will be physically tired, not so much from the distance covered or the weight drawn in the bow, though this is considerable, as from the controlled maintenance of steady effort while he is achieving refinement of aim and concentrating on technique while using a bow suited to his strength.

Even so, the physical effort does not of course compare with that expended in some other sports, but the degree of mental concentration can scarcely be matched in any other sporting activity. The archer is under his highest physical strain at the same time as he is mentally controlling his co-ordination and decision. He must strive to concentrate to his fullest capacity in spite of distractions without becoming anxious about his shooting. He must concentrate to such an extent as to obliterate what is going on around him, and to ignore what happened to the last arrow he shot (whether badly or well) in his determination to shoot the next one perfectly–once, that is, that he has decided what modifications to make, if any. Every item of his equipment must be constantly under review and every variation in weather conditions noted. He must be constantly alert and yet at no time should he become nervous, jumpy or irritable.

In competitive archery the strain is naturally greater, for added to the above are his feelings of responsibility to his team, his desire to shoot to the best of his ability with every shot and the knowledge he may have of the scores of close rivals (often displayed on a leader board). Yet even when there is no formal competition the archer is always fighting a battle–a personal battle inside himself. He is fighting to demonstrate his control of himself and his equipment, and if he fails to achieve what he knows he is capable of, he knows he can blame no one but himself– it's his own equipment, he maintains it, and no opportunities are given to him or withheld from him by opponents. Although archery can be made into a team sport, it is this essential loneliness while in the act of shooting that is part of its fascination.

Archery makes a wide appeal to all ages and conditions. Now that high-performance bows are available in a great variety of draw-weights and sizes, there is no reason why one should be unreasonably handicapped by youth or age. More is being done for juniors in schools and clubs and the best of our juniors are in fact challenging the best of adult archers. As in other sports, like swimming, it seems very likely that a high degree of skill can be achieved at an early age. On the other hand, archery can be learnt successfully in maturity and persisted in into advanced age. There are many instances of able archers holding their place in top competition in their sixties, and continuing to shoot quite well even in their eighties.

Nor does physical handicap necessarily prevent anyone taking up archery. Archery was introduced to paraplegics originally to strengthen the arms and encourage balance control, but it soon became clear that they could compete not only against each other, as in the Stoke Mandeville Games and the Paralympics, but also in open competition against able-bodied archers. Even more severe cases of injury have been overcome. I have had the pleasure of qualifying two tetraplegics as archery instructors, and I have seen a girl shooting with the feet alone, being totally unable to use her arms. Handicapped archers are welcome in most clubs. Their disability presents few problems and the fact that they are often nimble and adept with the fingers may benefit the club which they may serve as tackle maintenance officers, or as secretary or treasurer. The fact that they may be an asset and not a liability is of value to them as well as to the club.

One challenge that all archers have to meet is that of the weather, particularly in this country with its variable climate. To maintain one's standard of shooting throughout the heat of the day demands determination; to endure cold and rain and strong winds takes courage and patience. I have known tournaments abandoned or declared when the target faces started to disintegrate in the rain, or when the field became inches deep in water, but usually archers shoot on, whatever the conditions, taking shelter under umbrellas or in the miniature tents that are becoming a feature of our shooting lines. Those who shot in the 2nd All-British and Open Field Championships will remember that all types of British weather had to be endured and coped with, including rain, hail showers, strong blustery winds and bright sunshine. We are not all fair-weather archers. Some of us, very sensibly and fortunately, can get indoor shooting in suitable halls during the winter, but others shoot all the year round undaunted even by snow (though it is as well not to miss the target in such conditions!) At all times there is the effort to gain complete control of one's equipment—I hesitate to say mastery, for the ideal situation comes when the archer feels that the bow is an extension of himself and that he and his tackle are working in perfect conjunction. To this end, many archers are always experimenting, changing their bows for new models, for heavier or lighter weights, deciding to use longer or shorter arrows, experimenting with different shapes and materials by way of fletchings and buying the latest gimmicks. Granted the equipment must be right and that one certainly cannot shoot efficiently with a bow that is too heavy to control, all too often the fault lies with the archer rather than with the equipment. A good archer can shoot well with almost any tackle, but he will shoot best with that which is best suited to his own particular physique and technique. The search for this ideal combination is a constant challenge and inspiration.

Not surprisingly, a good many archers choose to make their own equipment, including composite bows. The best of these are as good as the best of professional bows, if not better, but to make such bows requires a high degree of skill and experience. There is great satisfaction in using equipment that one has made oneself, even when it may be not quite as good as one could buy–a sweet-shooting composite with a good mark at 100 yards, say, or a well-matched set of field arrows.

Finally, the sternest challenge the archer has to face is that of loss of form. At first the beginner will make steady progress and increased confidence will come with increased skill, but there will inevitably come a time when a plateau is reached. This is where perseverance and determination are needed and the help of a good coach is invaluable. To attempt to copy the styles of other successful archers, if these are peculiar, is not advisable, for what suits one archer may not suit another, and unless one copies all the technical points used by an expert one is liable to run into trouble. A better plan is to check over the basic technique, point by point, in an effort to find where inconsistency has crept in. All good archers are consistent, no matter how peculiar their style may appear to others. The challenge to each archer is to find a style that enables him to achieve this consistency himself.

Chapter 2

Taking it up

Undoubtedly it is best to join an archery club since here you will be provided with facilities, competent instruction and the encouragement that comes from associating with enthusiastic people with identity of interests. There is no substitute for the stimulus that comes from shooting with such people and debating and discussing archery points with them. Moreover, most clubs have a small stock of beginners' equipment which may be loaned free or at a low charge to prospective members. In this way you may be enabled to learn to shoot and develop a good technique before undertaking the expense of purchasing your own equipment. When the initial training period is over you will be in a better position to know what is a suitable type and weight of bow and a suitable length of arrow for you to buy. You will also be able to profit from the advice of more experienced archers regarding suitable tackle. The address of your nearest club secretary can be obtained on enquiry from the Secretary of the Grand National Archery Society or, probably, from the information department of your local library or local office of the Central Council of Physical Recreation.

There are over 600 clubs in Britain, but if you are so unfortunate as to find that there is none in your immediate vicinity, you may apply for one of the courses in archery laid on by the C.C.P.R., Further Education Departments, or other organisations whose purpose is to interest beginners in outdoor or indoor sporting pursuits. I say indoor, because it is quite possible to shoot indoors provided that a hall at least 25 yards long can be hired. Target archery clubs try to find such indoor accommodation during the winter months, though many archers shoot outdoors all the year round.

If, after reading the above, you are still driven back to practising archery on your own, it is quite possible to shoot in your own garden if it is large enough, or on some convenient piece of private ground you have permission to use. But you must be particularly careful about safety in this case. The direction of shooting must be such that there is no possibility of danger to any other person whether on your own ground or that adjoining it. Members of archery clubs that are affiliated to the G.N.A.S. are covered by Public Liability Insurance while official shooting is in progress, but even they are not covered when practising on their own premises away from the club.

If you are determined to shoot on your own, and have the necessary facilities, you can read the relevant chapters in this book on equipment and, in accordance with the advice given, purchase your own from one of the specialist archery suppliers who are also willing to give suitable advice to beginners. Then, by following the schemes of instruction outlined, you will be able to teach yourself on sound lines. Should you later have the opportunity to obtain coaching or to join a club, you will find that what you have already learnt will be in step with the general principles followed. Lastly, take an archery magazine: archery is an international sport attracting an ever-increasing number of participants and a magazine will widen your own sphere of interest immeasurably.

Equipment

Initially we will confine our attention to the essential tackle, leaving until later the additional equipment which may be found useful. Essentially one needs a bow, arrows, bracer and tab, a target to shoot at, and advisably a ground quiver on which to rest the bow and support the arrows when not in actual use. The prices of these vary enormously from the modest cost of practice tackle to the very high cost of some tournament equipment. All can be home-made by the enthusiastic amateur who has some skill in using tools and the willingness to take minute care with small details of construction. But home-made equipment is not necessarily cheaper than bought tackle when one considers the time taken and the likelihood of early mistakes, often costly in the case of bow construction. Generally, those who success-fully make equipment are those who already have wide experience of archery and appreciate fully the factors that must be considered. There-fore, it is advisable that you purchase your first set of practice tackle, unless you join a club where beginners' tackle is on loan.

Bows

The bow is in fact a machine that stores energy until it is required to be released. Ideally it should be easy to draw, easy to hold steady, and yet shoot with great speed of cast and steadiness. To get all these qualities in one bow is the aim of bowyers and at best they have to accept a compromise. For example, it is relatively easy to make a very fast bow, or to make a very steady bow, but to make a bow that has a fast cast and steadiness as well is a highly skilled craft.

Primitive bows were made of wood or whatever materials were available locally. But the disadvantage of wooden bows is that they tend to 'follow the string', or assume a set curve after continued use, which indicates that their efficiency has been reduced. One of the reasons for using yew as a bow-wood was that it was possible to use the natural qualities to best advantage. The yew-bow was constructed so that the pale sap-wood which resisted extension was used on the back of the bow, while the darker heart-wood which resisted compression was used on the belly side of the bow. In this way a more efficient weapon was evolved, but even so the cast of a yew-bow was relatively slow and a heavy draw-weight was required to enable a man to shoot successfully at long ranges.

The Turks gained a similar effect by laminating, with great skill, bows made of sinew, wood and horn. Their efficiency is hardly surpassed today, but such bows could never be a commercial proposition. The major break-through in modern times has been the introduction of fibre-glass to bow construction. Fibre-glass, being resistant to both extension and compression, has been found ideal for laminations on both the back and the belly of bows, giving the modern tournament bow its fine shooting qualities. Fibre-glass is also easy to control within fine limits during production. The manufacture of composite bows using fibre-glass is, however, still highly skilled, and gluing, even with highly efficient modern epoxy-resin glues, is a delicate process, so they are not cheap.

Beginners' practice bows are made relatively cheaply, though, of solid fibre-glass moulded to shape. They do not have the efficiency of laminated bows, because only part of the fibre-glass is stressed, but they have the merits of being virtually indestructible, very steady in action, maintaining their shooting qualities almost indefinitely and having a good resale value.

18

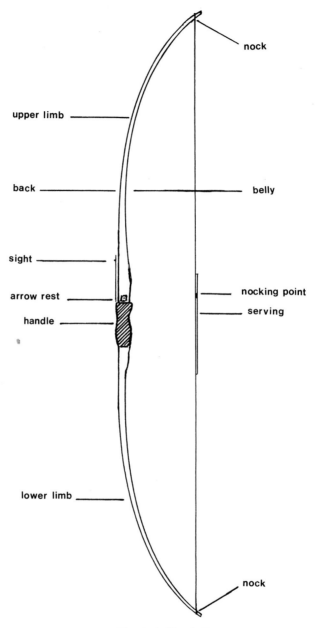

Fig. 1. A Simple Bow.

A bow should be suited to the height and strength of the archer using it, but a solid fibre-glass bow, drawing 28 lbs at 28 ins. could be used for initial practice by a wide variety of archers, since the shorter the archer, the less draw-weight he will use. Such a bow under-drawn by two inches will lose maybe four pounds of draw-weight. A bow of this weight will serve very well for practice, since the beginner will be able to achieve good control and a good technique. Later, a man may use a bow of 38 to 42 lbs draw-weight, and a lady one of 26 to 34 lbs, but such figures can only be approximate since individuals vary so much in length of arm and strength. The great thing is not to attempt to use a very heavy bow while one is learning the technique. In fact, one should guard against becoming over-bowed at any time. It is no use having a powerful bow that one cannot control.

Without going into too much detail it is as well to mention here some of the parts of the bow. There is the handle on which the hand is placed without gripping it tightly. Above and below the handle are the risers which strengthen the centre section and prevent it from bending. Where the risers merge into the working part of the limbs are the fade-outs. At the ends of the bow are the nocks into which the loops of the string fit when the bow is braced. The inside of the bow, that which faces the archer when it is drawn, is known as the face or belly; while the outer surface of the bow, that furthest from the archer, is called the back. There is a shelf or rest on which the arrow lies when drawn. Sights of various types may be added.

The string is made of Dacron sufficiently strong to withstand the shock of the bow when loosed. It will have a loop at the top. At the bottom it will have another loop, or, in the case of traditional long bows, a timber hitch for adjustment. The central part of the string will be served with nylon thread to protect it from any wear caused by chafing the bracer or by the use of the fingers, and a nocking point so placed that the arrow lies at right-angles to the string when it is placed on the rest. It may be found advantageous to have the nocking point $\frac{1}{8}$ in. or so above the right-angle. The nock of the arrow should fit snugly on the nocking point, so that it does not need to be held in place, yet can be released easily when shot.

Arrows

Until comparatively recently, arrows have been made of wood, because it is readily available, easily fashioned and expendable. With care one can select shafts of well-seasoned straight-grained wood that will individually make good arrows, but the important factor in all archery is the uniformity of the arrows in a set. This is difficult to achieve with wood, since it is a natural material and has the variability inherent in natural products. Each arrow in a set should have the same weight, the same point of balance and fletching, and the same spine or stiffness. It was in the effort to ensure a measure of uniformity of spine that the G.N.A.S. Spine Rating was instituted. If the shaft is supported at the extremities and a $1\frac{1}{2}$ lb. weight is hung on the centre, the shaft will bend. This deflection is measured in one-hundredths of an inch, so an arrow which deflects 60 one-hundredths of an inch is said to have a spine of 60 G.N.A.S. units. But this does not take account of the springiness factor of the shaft, or the speed of its return to normal when released from a bent position. It does, however, serve as a rough guide to the uniformity of shafts of the same material. Generally speaking, a fast bow requires a stiffish arrow, and a slow-shooting bow a whippier arrow. If the arrow is not matched to the bow it will not shoot well.

With all these considerations in mind, it will be readily appreciated that a well-matched set of wooden arrows would be hard and expensive to make. Fortunately for the modern archer, high-grade alloy tubing is now manufactured and processed for arrow construction. This can be controlled at all stages of production so that a tournament set of arrows can be certified to be practically identical in every respect. Apart from the guaranteed tensile strength of the shaft material, the tube dimensions can be etched on each shaft as follows: 1816. This would mean that the shaft is 18 sixty-fourths overall diameter, and 16 thousandths wall thickness. In this way a great variety of sets can be made to ensure suitability to any bow on the market and any archer's peculiarity of technique and draw-length. As in all archery you pay for what you get. Tubular fibre-glass arrows are available too, and have the quality of being very unlikely ever to take a set or permanent bend. But for beginners, quite cheap sets of beginners' practice alloy arrows are available, well constructed and durable and quite well matched for the price.

The most important part of the arrow assembly is the fletching. Unless fletchings are put on correctly the arrow will not fly true. Traditionally, feathers have been used for the purpose and they are still in use, being inexpensive and durable. But owing to shortage of natural feathers, plastic fletching is becoming more common. Feather fletchings must be well-matched, that is to say, they must be cut from the same part of the wing-quill of feathers of similar quality and the same wing of the bird. The primary feathers on the left wing of a bird are the reverse shape from those on the right. If mixed left and right wing fletchings were used on a shaft, it could not fly true. Even when feather fletchings are put straight along the shaft, the characteristics of the feathers impart a spiral twist into the movement of the shaft in flight. Obviously this is advantageous, helping to steer the arrow more effectively, as the rifling in a rifle causes rotation to a bullet. This effect can be increased by offsetting the fletching by 2 degrees or so.

Plastic vanes are also widely used by more proficient archers, and these must be offset, as the shaft will not rotate if they are put on straight. As regards the number of fletchings on a shaft, beginners' arrows have three. It may be found later that an archer will prefer four-fletch, but three-fletch is quite satisfactory. With three-fletched arrows, one feather, called the cock-feather, is set at right-angles to the slot of the nock, and the others at 120 degrees to it and to each other. This cock-feather is usually of a different colour from the others, so as to be easily recognisable, because it is important that the arrow be nocked onto the string in such a way that the cock-feather does not brush against the bow when shot.

It is as well if the fletchings are set fairly well back on the shaft provided that they do not get in the way of the fingers on the string. Their size is important. If they are too small they will not hold the shaft on course; if they are too large they will impart too much drag. The height of the fletching is more important than the length, however.

Length of arrow is another important consideration. If an arrow is used that is too short for the archer, he will be cramped and unable to open his shoulders to the required extent, or he will be in danger of drawing the arrow inside the bow with the likelihood of damaging the arrow and injuring himself. Therefore, it is generally recommended that the novice use an arrow which is an inch or so too long for him. It will shoot quite well and he will be in no danger of over-drawing. One can only measure an archer accurately for arrow-length after he has settled down to a consistent style of shooting and even then only by taking an average of observed draw-lengths in the actual bow he intends to use. But a rough guide for the beginner can be arrived at by getting him to extend both arms forward and measuring the distance from the top of the breast-bone to the tips of his out-stretched fingers as in Fig. 2. An arrow an inch or two longer than this is safe for a beginner to use for initial practice.

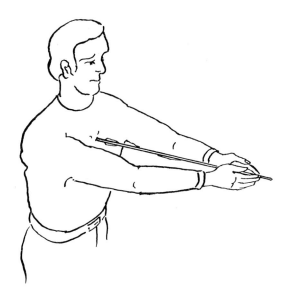

Fig. 2. A Safe Length of Arrow.

Bracers

It is sometimes stated that the bracer is a substantial arm-guard of leather designed to protect the archer's arm from the slap of the string. This is erroneous. If the bow is held and shot correctly the string will not touch the arm or bracer, except perhaps lightly after loosing with a relaxed hold. No, its primary purpose is to keep loose clothing out of the way of the string. Consequently there is no need for it to be unduly thick or bulky. For quick change where beginners are sharing bracers there are several designs, but for individual use, the best designs incorporate three straps of leather or elastic with suitable easily adjusted fittings. The bracer should cover the inside of the fore-arm above and below the bracing height of the bow and not chafe either the wrist or the elbow joint. Since it must fit neatly and not bulge, some designs incorporate a thin strip of plastic or metal to preserve its shape. Some are moulded to the shape of the fore-arm and cover the elbow joint, but these are not really necessary, except for bows that have an extremely high bracing height or with advanced styles that involve locking the elbow. A simple home-made design is shown in Chapter 12.

Tabs

Again, it might be thought that the purpose of the tab is to protect the fingers from soreness occasioned by holding and loosing the string. This, too, is a mistaken idea. The tab is used to provide a loosing surface that is smooth and consistent. The uncovered fingers are liable to be affected by sweating causing an inconstant loose. Pony crupp butt has been the traditional material for tabs and it is still very reliable, but the use of hair tabs and tabs made of man-made materials is increasing. Hair tabs give a smooth loose under any weather conditions, even rain. Some archers complain of soreness between the fingers occasioned by pinching the arrow and purchase tabs provided with a block intended to keep the first two fingers apart, but the finger tips can still slide together and in any case pinching is caused by a fault in technique. The beginner will find a simple pony butt or Corfam tab quite satisfactory.

However, the shape and size is important. In many ways the tab is the most individual part of the archer's equipment and must be tailored to fit. It will not always be found possible to purchase a made tab that can conveniently be trimmed – for instance, the finger-holes may be too large. The best plan is to cut a tab out of cheap off-cut leather of suitable suppleness and thickness and experiment until the ideal shape and size has been arrived at, and then to cut a superior tab out of a square of pony butt. When doing this, take care to observe the grain of the leather. It is necessary to ensure that the grain runs length-wise along the fingers as, if this is not done, the tab will soon curl up and fail to give a clean loose. Leather will stretch more across the grain than along it.

Now, shape. The tab must be securely fixed over one or more fingers of the drawing-hand, preferably two to avoid swivelling. The tab must cover the first three fingers of the string-hand, but must not extend further than the finger tips. There should be no spare leather above the forefinger which will give a false impression of anchoring under the chin. And the slot must be wide enough to avoid pinching the arrow between the first two fingers. The design in Chapter 12 will be found to be of suitable size for the average hand.

Shooting-gloves are sometimes advocated, but it is not easy to get a clean loose when all the three shooting fingers are enclosed. A thin leather glove with tips attached is better, but this really needs to be strapped back to the hand so that it does not creep forward. Even so, the likelihood is that the archer will hook his fingers unduly when using a glove, so a well-made tab is recommended.

Some archers apply talcum-powder or french chalk to the tab to ensure a slippery surface, but this is not advisable, for when the talc has been freshly applied the loose will be faster than it will be when it has worn off to some extent, and the performance of the arrow will vary. Moreover, if the tab should get wet in rain, powder will matt and congeal and produce a sticky, gluey surface that is the last thing an archer wants. A good tab made of the right material will shoot well in most conditions that one is likely to meet.

Ground Quivers

The essential features of a ground quiver are that it should provide a secure support for the bow when not in use at a suitable height from the ground, and a means of holding arrows ready to hand when they are about to be used without fouling the fletchings. Provided it does this, can be easily pushed into the ground, and is not too bulky to be packed away with one's tackle, it serves its purpose very well. It is a convenience for packing if the top section can be dismantled, but this is not essential.

Chapter 3

Safety & Etiquette

So far archery has proved to be one of the safest sports. Paradoxically this may be because the potentiality of the bow to cause injury is fairly obvious. Consequently rules to ensure safety on the range have been drawn up and so long as these are followed there is little likelihood of danger. In fact the very few accidents that have come to my notice have been the result of failure to observe the rules. Even experienced archers need to be reminded of safety rules, because one tends to get rather casual as confidence grows.

Safety rules are designed not only for those concerned with handling the tackle or preparing it for use, but also for those involved in an organised meeting.

Handling Tackle

Beginners should always have impressed upon them the fact that a bow is not a toy, but a potentially lethal weapon. That is particularly important with juniors for it might be thought that junior bows, being less powerful than those used by adults, are not particularly dangerous. This is a fallacy. Even a light bow can deliver an arrow with sufficient force to penetrate corrugated iron, and a heavy arrow with a suitable head shot from a powerful bow will have more penetrating power than a bullet from a revolver or even, under certain conditions, than a rifle. Consequently, a loaded bow should not be drawn except on the shooting line and in the direction of the target. A drawn bow should not be pointed at anyone, even without an arrow on the string, the reason being that the person aimed at cannot see the bow is not loaded and may move into danger in order to avoid it. There is also the chance that the bow may break and the pieces fly forwards.

Unbreakable solid fibre-glass bows are best for beginners' use. Even if drawn beyond their stated recommended draw-length they will not break, but archers should never draw a bow beyond its intended limit. Habits of careless handling of solid fibre-glass bows could be continued when a laminated bow is used, with disastrous results.

A bow should never be loosed from full-draw without an arrow for fear of breaking the bow. The arrow, though very light, has imparted to it the power of the bow which is not designed to withstand the shock of recoil when it is loosed without an arrow. For the same reason, strings should always be inspected before use so that the archer does not suffer the misfortune of having one break while the bow is being used, risking damage to the bow. Any string with a broken strand or showing signs of fraying should be discarded.

When bracing a bow care should be taken to ensure that it cannot slip and injure the archer, and that the string is firmly located in the nocks and along the string-groove. Composite bows should not be braced by the 'step-in' method for fear of twisting the limbs. Done properly this method is all right, but so few archers do it properly that they are well advised to use the simple 'push-pull' method or to use a bow-stringer or to enlist the help of another archer to slip the string loop over the top nock while the owner bends the bow.

One should be cautious about lending one's bow to another archer – it may not be suitable. As for arrows, check alloys for straightness and fletching; and if using wooden arrows for any reason be on the look-out for cracks or lifting of the grain.

It is advisable for beginners to use arrows 1 in. to 2 ins. too long so as to prevent any arrow being drawn inside the bow. Since young people grow rapidly it is as well to make a frequent check on the length of arrows being used by juniors, especially if they are their own property. Club arrows should not be provided in more than two, or maybe three, standard lengths, and each length should be clearly distinguishable to avoid confusion, preferably by differently coloured cresting bands. Some manufacturers have standardised the fletching colours in accordance with lengths of practice arrows, and this is a good idea, but not invariably followed as yet. Bracers should always be worn to keep sleeves out of the way of the string and to afford some measure of protection in the case of a bad shot. Sleeves should be rolled down and strapped under the bracer. If rolled up, they become more likely to foul the string.

Clothing

Loose clothing which might foul the string should not be worn. Ties should be removed or tucked inside the shirt or pullover. Metal badges, jewellery or strings of beads that might foul the string should be removed.

Shooting Procedure

After shooting, archers should not run up to the targets, but should walk, eyes down, to the side of the target, so that arrows that have fallen short are not trodden on nor allowed to cause a lacerated ankle. When arrows are withdrawn, archers must not stand in front of the target, risking being struck in the eye by a nock as the shaft is being withdrawn. The archer drawing the shaft should ensure that no one is in a position of danger.

The archer must never shoot straight up, except in Popinjay where special arrows are used and special safety provisions are in force, for the arrow will disappear from view and wind currents may take it in unexpected directions.

At an Organized Meeting

Archers other than those actually shooting should remain at least 5 yards behind the shooting line. Archers should not go up to the targets, nor should shooting recommence except on the signal of the person in charge – the coach or field captain. A whistle code in common use is one blast to commence shooting; two blasts to move forward to score and collect arrows; and a series of short blasts to demand a cease-fire when for any reason it is necessary to interrupt the shooting. It is the duty of anyone who sees cause for the shooting to stop in the interests of safety to shout 'Fast!', the traditional order to archers to stop shooting and come down.

Spectators should be kept at least 15 yards behind and at least 10 yards away from the ends of the shooting line. Obviously they should not be allowed to encroach on the ends of the target line. In a tournament it is as well if the whole area is roped off with ample provision for safety and warning flags flown.

Targets should be so spaced and sited that there is no chance of a passer-by or a participant in another sport passing anywhere near the fall of the arrows. Ample overshot must be allowed behind the targets and ample space at the sides, say 50 yards beyond and 30 yards at the sides. It should be realized that when beginners are shooting at close range they need more overshot than experienced archers shooting at long range, since an arrow going over the top of the target will travel farther before it strikes ground. There is also the point that in dry weather arrows that miss the target are liable to skid long distances. For the above reasons it is a good practice to move the targets towards the archers at a change of distance, rather than for the archers to move forward, unless there is plenty of overshot anyway.

Targets should be securely fixed to the stand and the stand to the ground. Even a moderate wind can overthrow a target and smash every arrow in it. A target full of bent and buckled arrows is one of the saddest sights to see, even if yours are not among them. Through some malicious dispensation of fate, such disasters always seem to happen when brand-new arrows are in use!

The number of archers shooting at one time on each target should be restricted so as to avoid unreasonable cross-fire; as many as 6 archers could shoot in two details of 3, but this is about the limit.

In Field Archery where the targets are not likely to be visible except from the particular shooting stations, special care must be taken. The whole area should be marked off, warning notices posted, steps taken to ensure that the public do not trespass but remain in the allocated safe spectator areas, and the route for the archers to follow clearly indicated. Obviously no shots should be set in the direction either of another target or of the paths along which the archers will walk. This calls for careful planning on the part of those setting the course. There is also the chance of an arrow striking a tree and being deflected, so shots should be reasonably clear and targets kept a safe distance from each other. When field archers collect arrows which may have fallen behind the target it is necessary to ensure that a following group do not begin shooting thinking that the target is clear. One useful practice is to lay a bow across the target face as an indication that a party is still engaged in a search.

Furthermore, no one should take a shot at a bird or beast that might come into view on a target shoot or field shoot. Humanitarian reasons apart, it is a dangerous practice since there is a tendency to follow the quarry as it moves and to concentrate one's whole attention on it.

Photographers should not be allowed to distract archers and certainly not take photographs from in front of the line. With modern equipment it is quite possible to get good action shots from behind the 5-yard line and without distracting the archer in any way. Photographers who do not realise the danger have been known to persuade an archer to pose with the arrow drawn straight towards the photographer. This may produce a dramatic picture; it could also produce a dead photographer.

Etiquette

Although the following observances do not relate directly to safety, they are so closely associated with conduct at a shoot that it seems appropriate to include them here. These are not compulsory as some of the safety observances are, but as a matter of courtesy and consideration for others they should be followed no less strictly:

Be independent and don't expect others to dance attendance on you.
Always keep a spare string and spare arrows. If you do have to borrow any tackle, return it in good condition or replace it or pay for it if damaged.
Do not touch another's tackle without permission.
Wait till all arrows have been scored before going behind the target to retrieve arrows.
It is a kindly act to collect arrows for a disabled archer if he wishes it. It may, however, sometimes be more courteous to allow him to collect his own rather than be too helpful.
If you break another archer's arrow by carelessness (e.g. by treading on it when it is clearly visible) pay for it in cash on the spot. Accidental damage to arrows in the target in the course of shooting is just bad luck on the owner.
Don't keep everyone waiting an unreasonable length of time while you look for a lost arrow, but be prepared to help make a quick search.
Call your score clearly and correctly.
Comparing scores up and down the line is very bad form. Keep quiet about your score and neither grouse nor boast.
Vacate your place on the line as soon as you have finished shooting, but do not suddenly move while someone next to you is about to shoot. If an archer suffers a broken bow-string, it is a courtesy to stay on the line to prevent the Field Captain from whistling up if the archer has more arrows to shoot at the end.
Don't stay on the line gazing through binoculars at your last arrow. An

archer is entitled to shoot at the speed that suits him (within limits), but there should be no delay in moving off or on to the line.

Stand well back from the shooting line and converse quietly. Loud voices and laughter can be very distracting. Some people prefer not to talk at all. Leave them in peace.

Thank the target captain and lieutenant at the end of the shoot.

Don't leave litter.

If you must bring pets or small children to a shoot, keep them under control and don't allow them to disturb other archers.

If you wish to photograph an archer in action it is courteous to ask him first if he minds. It might put him off.

Chapter 4

Learning to Shoot: Target

Assuming for some reason you are unable to get initial instruction from a qualified person, the next best thing is to learn the 'Basic' technique yourself by carefully following what is set down in this chapter. This 'Basic' technique is the one on which all G.N.A.S. Instructors and Coaches are trained, so if at some future time you want coaching you will already have a good foundation.

First set up your target 20 yards away.

The Dominant or Controlling Eye

The first thing is to check if you have a dominant or controlling eye, because most people develop the habit of using one eye more than the other, just as the majority use one hand more than the other, and since in archery the nock of the arrow needs to be positioned vertically below the sighting eye it is important to ensure the correct eye is being used. In general the right-handed person will also have a controlling right eye, and some left-handed persons a controlling left eye. For the purpose of archery this presents no problem, but for the exception to this rule a little attention is needed to make certain the person concerned is not at a disadvantage.

One simple method of checking if you have a controlling eye is to look at a small object a few yards away, the gold centre of the target will do, and then point to it with an outstretched arm, with the index finger extended. Then close one eye, open it, and close the other eye, noting whether in doing so the object appears to move to one side; if so, the eye closed is the controlling one. Should it be the right eye and you are right-handed in other things, the bow will be held in the left hand. If it is the left eye and you are left-handed the bow will be held in the right hand. In either case there is no particular need to close or cover the non-controlling eye while you are shooting.

Should the controlling eye be the opposite one to your normal hand you can still follow the above directions, but you will have to close, or cover, the controlling eye and make the non-controlling eye do the work.

If you are ambidextrous you can let the controlling eye determine which hand holds the bow, or follow the directions given in the last paragraph. You may find you have no controlling eye; the object does not appear to move, or it appears to move whichever eye is closed. In this case you can hold the bow in either hand, but you must close, or cover, the unwanted eye; otherwise you may find one eye doing the necessary work and then, at some later stage, the other eye taking over, which will alter your view of the target, very much to the detriment of your shooting.

Having determined which hand holds the bow, you can put on your bracer, finger tab and quiver, and brace the bow. (Plate 1.) Now measure the distance between the centre of your sighting eye and the under edge of your jaw, and put a pencil mark on the bow face at the same distance above the arrow shelf. This will give you a mark to use when you come to aiming. If your bow has an adjustable sight you can move this up to the same position, instead of making a pencil mark. (Plate 2.)

Plate 1. Bracing the bow.   Plate 2. Setting the sight for initial practice.

Checking the Standing Position

For the sake of simplicity the instructions will be given as for a right-handed archer–bow in the left hand.

Put your bow on the ground quiver if you have one; failing this, lay it on the ground. Then take up a position astride the shooting line, and at right angles to it, bow arm towards the target, with your feet apart about the same width as your shoulders, body weight evenly distributed on both feet. The body should be upright but not tense. Allow the arms to hang loosely at your sides, and then, while looking straight ahead, lift your arms sideways to shoulder level. (Plate 3.) Now close your left eye and turn your head so that you can see the target over the bridge of your nose, and check if your hand is pointing to the vertical centre line of the target. If you are pointing to the left of centre, move your feet round a little in a clockwise direction, while looking at the target, until your

Plate 3. Establishing the standing position.

hand is pointing to the centre. If your hand is pointing to the right of centre, move your feet anti-clockwise. Now lower your arms to your sides, and do this checking movement again, remembering to look straight ahead until you have lifted your arms. This should make quite certain you have got the standing position right. You have now determined where your feet should be to position the body in the correct relationship to the target. You can now put down your foot markers.

Checking the Head Position

Take an arrow from the quiver and hold it upright against your face, just touching the tip of your nose and the centre of your chin, with the bottom end of the arrow clear of your chest. Close the left eye and turn your head until the upright arrow appears to cut down the centre of the target. Now without moving your head take the arrow away from your face, and you will have a clear view of the target over the bridge of your nose. This will help to register in your mind the correct head position for future reference without doing the complete check.

Holding the Bow and Positioning the Bow Arm

Pick up the bow in your left hand and let the bow arm hang down at your side, string uppermost, as though you were holding a small suit-case, with your thumb pointing up the centre of the bow face. Now move the thumb down to a normal holding position. The bow handle should be just held, never gripped. Without in any way altering the bow hand lift the arm level with your shoulder, so that the bow is horizontal to the ground. Now bring the bow into an upright position by turning your hand at the wrist. You should now see a clear space between the bow arm and string, which, provided you do not stiffen the bow arm by tensing the muscles, is how it should be when you are shooting. Now bring the bow arm down to the original position where it was hanging loosely at your side.

Nocking the Arrow

Move the bow arm forward bringing the bow in front of your body, about level with your waist, and horizontal to the ground. Take an arrow from your quiver, or ground quiver, whichever you are using, with the first two fingers and thumb of the shaft hand just below the fletchings. Lay the arrow across the bow, turn the arrow so that the cock-feather is pointing upwards, and push the nock well on to the nocking point.

There are many methods of nocking the arrow, but the one described is very simple, and gives you a clear view of what you are doing, and of whether the bracing height of the string remains constant.

Positioning the Fingers on the String

Without moving the bow from its position in front of the body bring it to a slight angle by turning the bow hand, anti-clockwise, at the wrist. Extend the open shaft hand, with the palm facing upwards, towards the string and at right angles to it. Place the second and third fingers on the string to the left of the arrow with a small space between the edge of the second finger and the arrow, one-eighth of an inch will do. The string should lie in the first crease of both fingers, and, since these two fingers are rarely the same length, you will probably have to bend the second finger a little more than the third finger to bring the two creases in line with the string. Take a little bow weight on these two fingers by drawing the string an inch or so, and you should now find the ends of both fingers can be crooked upwards, and the string is then firmly held by the pads that build up in front of the string, while the rest of the fingers and palm are almost straight. Still holding the bow slightly drawn place the first finger on the string to the right of the arrow, and just touching it. (Plate 4.) Now let the string return to its normally undrawn position, and by looking down at your shaft arm you should see that it forms one straight line with the arrow. (Plate 5.)

Plate 4. Fingers on the string.   Plate 5. The Preparation position.

Practising the Loose

You have now completed most of the preparation to shooting, but to help you appreciate what should happen when you loose an arrow a little practice, before coming to full draw, is desirable.

Draw the bow about six to eight inches by parting the hands. Hold this position a few seconds and then draw the shaft arm another inch, and, at the same time, straighten the fingers. The arrow will quickly leave the bow and stick in the ground a yard or two from where you are standing. Shoot a few arrows in this way, say four to six, by which time you should be able to do the loose, reasonably well, at full draw.

Preparing to Draw

Nock an arrow and position the fingers on the string, checking that the bow hand is correctly placed on the bow handle, just holding it but not gripping. Now check that the bow arm is extended without being tense or stiff, and the arrow and shaft arm form one long straight line, whether it is viewed from the top as you see it, or from the front as an onlooker would. Having seen these various things are correct, lift your head and look straight in front along the shooting line. You should now be standing quite upright, shoulders well down without muscular tension, body weight evenly distributed on both feet.

If your eye check indicated you need to close the left eye, do it now and then turn your head to the target, just as you did when checking the head position. Fix your gaze on the target centre, and from now on avoid looking directly at the bow or string. As you come to full draw the bow will be imposed on this sight line.

Coming to Full Draw

Extend the bow and string by separating the two hands, at the same time lifting the bow arm up and sideways to shoulder level, and the shaft arm, folded at the elbow, to the same level, the edge of the first finger underneath the jaw but not following the jaw line. (Plate 6.) While drawing the bow you should bring it into an upright position, by turning the bow hand at the wrist, allowing the shaft hand and arm to turn at the same rate, so that by the time the bow is upright it is also at full draw. As you do this movement with your arms you should have the feeling of pushing the bow hand forward, and pushing the shaft-arm elbow back. This will help you to use the right muscles.

Plate 6. Full Draw. Under-chin Anchor for Target Shooting.

Some people find it difficult at first to draw the bow, because it is an unaccustomed body movement. Instead of letting it be an equal effort across the body, they try to put extra effort in one arm, move more often than not the bow arm, or they change the head position, or move the body in some way. If you have any such difficulty, practise drawing the bow a few times without an arrow on the string, and you will soon master it.

At the full draw the string should just touch the centre of the nose and chin. In the first instance you may find it is not touching your nose. If so, take note of whether it is touching your chest. If it is, lift your bow hand a little, and drop the shaft arm elbow by the same amount, so finger pressures on the string are unchanged. If, however, the string is not touching your chest, tilt your head forward until your nose touches the string. Thereafter try to get your head in this position when you first turn your head to the target, before coming to full draw.

Beginners sometimes find that as they come to full draw the arrow drops off the shelf. This is because they are either turning the shaft hand a little faster than the bow, or bringing the shaft hand up to the jaw before the bow hand reaches shoulder level. If anything, let your bow hand slightly lead the other one, and you should have no trouble in this respect. If you have occasion to make any of the above adjustments, try to avoid looking at anything but the target, because it is of more value to feel what you are doing, to get things right, than to watch what you are doing.

Aiming

Having come to full draw, you should see the target close to the left-hand side of the upright bow, partly obscured by the bow, with the string, out of focus, within the width of the bow limb. Normally you would not look at the string because this means altering the focus of your sighting eye, which should be on the target. However, if you find the string is to the left of the bow, it means you need to adjust your head position. This is done by tilting your head a little to the left, while still keeping the string on your nose and chin. Very slight adjustment will move the string within the bow limb, giving a clear view of the target.

You should now note where the pencil mark, or sight, is in relation to the target's horizontal centre line, and if it is above, bring it down to this line by a slight sideways movement of your body to the left from the waist, keeping the hips and legs quite still. If the sight is below the centre line, the slight body movement should be to the right. The sight having been brought to the right target level, it should also appear to be poised somewhere between the outside edges of the gold centre. You need not try to hold it at too exact a point in that area. You are now on aim, but this should never be the signal to loose the arrow.

Holding

Up to this point you have followed a pattern of movement that could by practice become almost automatic, but from now on you should take your time to sense everything is as it should be, and you and the bow are steady. You should also feel that the effort of holding the bow on aim is in the muscles extending along the back of your arms to the point where the shoulder blades are cushioning against each other. The emphasis is on feeling the right muscles are being used without thinking about it, and you may at first find it difficult to get this feeling, largely because your attention is concentrated on the target. If you closed your eyes for a few seconds you would quickly realise the feeling was there, and whether it was in the right place, or not. Closing your eyes is not something you would normally do, because it breaks your attention to the target, but just done as an initial test it could certainly help you to get the right feeling.

If you feel that anything is wrong with your holding position, bring the bow down to the preparatory position and start again. Having satisfied yourself all is well, you are now ready to loose the arrow.

Loosing

While keeping your attention on the target, with the sight, a little out of focus, aimed at the gold, put a bit more pushing effort in the shaft-arm elbow and straighten the fingers of the shaft hand at the same time. This is to ensure the string leaves the fingers at, or near, the chin. The loosing action should be a smooth easy one, without any kind of snatch or jerk. See Plate 7. The best kind of loose is one that apparently happens at the right moment, something you feel without thinking about it. But this can only come by diligent practice. This practice will be made much more effective if, after coming on aim, you close your eyes and feel what happens to the shaft hand when you loose. It should be felt to move

Plate 7. The Loose.

quickly back, with the edge of the first finger sliding along the forward part of the jaw. This again is something you would not normally do while shooting, but for practice purposes it can be very effective, and will help you to appreciate the feeling of a good, or bad, loose, when you come to shoot normally.

Follow Through

Until the arrow has reached the end of its flight there should be no movement of any part of the body other than the reflex movements consequent upon losing the draw weight of the bow, by loosing the string off the fingers, the bow hand moving a little towards the target, and the shaft hand in the opposite direction. During the first part of this follow-through period, while the arrow is still on the string, the bow is not only propelling the arrow forward, it is also guiding it in the direction you wish it to follow. Hence the need to maintain the bow in its on-aim position.

During the follow-through you may find there is a temptation to look for the arrow in flight. You should avoid this by keeping the focus of your sighting eye firmly on the target, and provided the light is reasonably good the arrow will come into view on, or near, the target. After you have shot three arrows retire from the shooting line, and rest for a few minutes before shooting again. This is part of Shooting Rules, and a wise one, because it helps prevent physical and mental tiredness, and assists you to shoot your last arrow as well as your first. When you go up to the shooting line again make certain you position your feet correctly to the foot markers.

After you have shot your second three arrows put your bow on the ground quiver, and then go up to the target to collect your arrows. Do not hurry in case there is an arrow, or arrows, sticking in the ground in front of the target. Look out for such arrows to avoid walking into them, which could injure you, and damage the arrows. Having reached the target, take careful note of where your arrows have landed; high or low on the target; or perhaps just over the target; and whether they are grouped together. Now withdraw the arrows, one at a time. By placing one hand flat against the target face with the arrow between thumb and first finger, and grasping the arrow with the other hand close to the target, draw the arrow out taking care not to bend it. You may find it more convenient to place the back of the hand against the target so that the thumb is free to retain the arrows as they are drawn.

Correcting the Aim

On returning from the target and taking up your position on the shooting line you should now make any necessary correction to the position of the bow sight. This is done by holding the bow upright with the sight aimed at the target centre, noting the position on the bow relative to where the arrows actually landed, which indicates just how far, and in what direction, you need to move the bow sight to correct your aim. For example, if your arrows landed two rings low of the target centre, and this appears on the bow to be half an inch below the bow sight, you need to slide the bow sight down by half an inch, so that when you come on aim the bow will be lifted by the right amount to bring the arrows to the target centre. On the other hand, if the arrows landed two rings high, the bow sight would need to be slid up half an inch. You are now ready to continue your shooting practice.

Extending the Range

Once you have reached the stage where your arrows are grouping, very regularly, on the target, you can increase the range by moving the target back 10 yards. Your bow sight will need to be adjusted, but if you first shoot six arrows at the new distance, and take note how low they land on the target, you can then correct the bow sight by the method described earlier.

As your shooting progresses you can move the target further back, in stages of 10 yards at a time. For future reference put a pencil mark on the bow limb to indicate the position for the bow sight at these various distances. By careful practice you will soon be achieving good results at the longer distances. But bearing in mind that shooting in the bow is, probably, exercising your muscles in an unaccustomed way, it would be wise to avoid shooting for too long on the first few occasions. Set yourself a limit of three dozen arrows and the effect on the muscles will be minimised.

Chapter 5

Learning to Shoot: Field and Clout

What you have learnt by following the instructions given in the previous chapter has been the Basic Method of Target Archery. It may be that you will be entirely satisfied with the pleasure of shooting at targets at known distances over a flat field. If so, by all means persevere with it and leave Field Archery to those to whom it appeals. There are many archers, however, who practise and enjoy both. There are others again who specialise in Field Archery, finding the greater variety of shots and hazards and the moving from target to target over an interesting course in woodland or rough country more to their personal taste.

If you have started on Target Archery, I would recommend that you continue to practise it until you are thoroughly familiar with the technique. When this is established you can then try the other forms detailed in later chapters. Of these, the most popular is Field Archery. In some of its forms an adaptation of target style may be used, but if you wish to shoot instinctively you will find that once you have been in the habit of using a sight on the bow you will have to work hard to achieve a truly instinctive style. On the other hand, there is so much carry-over of technique in other respects that a knowledge of target basic will be decidedly beneficial.

I will attempt to deal with the teaching of both Freestyle and Barebow Field Archery. In Freestyle, sights may be used and usually are. In Barebow, no sights are allowed, but it is permissible to use the point of the arrow as an aiming aid. This is called using the 'space-picture'. If you ignore completely the picture of the bow and arrow in relationship to the target, but FEEL that you are directing your shot correctly at the target, you are shooting instinctively.

Shooting Freestyle

The distances at which field targets are set out may be marked or unmarked, but this makes no difference to the actual technique. The archer reads or estimates the distance, adjusts the sight, stands (or kneels) in the most comfortable and effective position for the shot, both feet behind the line indicated by the post from which he is to shoot, draws, anchors, aims and looses much as in target archery. But there are several points to remember.

1. Calibration

The bow must be correctly calibrated to match the arrows being used (for they may not be the same as those used for target shooting). To do this, set the sight for 10 yards (or for 10 metres if you are calibrating for metric rounds) and check it for accuracy by actually shooting at a field target over more or less level ground. When you are satisfied, mark the sight position, move the sight pin $\frac{1}{4}$ in. to $\frac{1}{2}$ in. down the bow, retire to 20 yards (or to 20 metres) and check this. Carry on setting the sights until you have a range from 10 to 60 yards (or metres). Then check the sights at all ranges including intermediate ones by shooting one arrow from each position, altering the sight to the marks you have made with due allowance for intermediate distances. You may find that the shorter distance marks may be slightly closer together than the longer distance marks. This would not be surprising, since, for the early part of its flight, the arrow follows a flatter trajectory than it does later.

2. Use of Sights

Naturally you will usually set the sights according to the distance known or estimated. But if you are shooting a steep uphill or downhill shot, you will have to allow for the angle. At short ranges it may not make much difference, but at longer ranges you will find that a downhill shot will tend to fly higher than otherwise expected, whereas an uphill shot will not be much changed, so bear that in mind in setting the sight, but do not overdo the allowance.

3. Standing

You will often be unable to stand in the orthodox target archer's position in relation to the target owing to uneven ground or overhanging branches. The essential thing is to stand in the most stable and comfortable position you can manage and to preserve the alignment of the shoulders to the target. Usually this will call for movement at the hips.

4. *Estimating the Distance*

Accuracy can only be achieved by constant practice. It is one thing to estimate the distance of a four-foot target on a flat field and quite another to judge the distance of a field target (which may be one of four sizes) in rough undulating country, over water, uphill or downhill, in shade or in brilliant sunlight, with foliage or bracken around to confuse your calculations. But one thing is certain. The more you do it, the better you'll get. It is some help if you can recognise the size of the target displayed because, if the course is correctly set out, that target will be set within certain limits of range.

5. *Observing the Shot*

Target archers are advised not to watch the arrow as it leaves the bow, but to continue to concentrate on the target. Well and good, the target archer is shooting a large number of arrows at the same distance and may use binoculars to spot his arrows. There is no harm in watching the arrow provided one does not affect the shot by doing so, but since the beginner is prone to do this, he is advised not to watch the arrow in flight. In field archery few shots are taken from one station, often only one, and binoculars may be used only in marked distance rounds. Therefore it is a help if you can observe the fall of the arrows— again provided that in so doing you do not jerk or snatch the shot or fail to maintain the follow-through. Adjustment of sight may be called for, as your previously estimated distance may have been incorrect. If you have missed the target, the arrow may have disappeared into the undergrowth if the target area is not well cleared. Even so it is possible to concentrate on the target and still be aware of the arrow flight at the same time. Most people have a moderately wide field of vision. If you are strongly dominant in the eye used for aiming, you may be able to aim satisfactorily with both eyes open as many field archers do. But if in shooting target style you have been obliged to keep the disengaged eye closed, then you will have to continue to do so and accept its limitations.

Shooting Barebow (With Space-picture)

We have seen that shooting freestyle is much like target archery in its technique except that the feet may be differently positioned. Much of the technique of shooting barebow is basically the same, too, but there

Plate 8. Full draw. Cheek anchor for Field Shooting.

are a few important modifications brought about by the absence of a sight or sight mark of any kind on the bow or on the string.

In aiming at the target with a sight, the target is kept in clear focus and the sight, though out of focus, is still visible against the target. If the target archer chose to take sufficient notice, he would find that while aiming on the target he could also see less distinctly the bow, the string and the arrow as well as a good deal of the surrounding countryside in peripheral vision. At short ranges the arrow pile would appear to be pointing well below the target, because the nock of the arrow below his chin is also well below eye level. But if he had a means of aligning his arrow-pile with some mark on the ground in the right relationship to the target he could shoot accurately without the aid of the sight. This is in effect what the point-of-aim field archer does. From his experience of the power of his bow over known distances he places the point of the arrow on some part of the target, or below it or above it according to the distance at which he estimates the target to be set. It is very important, of course, that he should be extremely consistent in draw-length and in loosing technique. If, instead of selecting a mark to point at before drawing, he draws and then judges the space between the centre of the target and where he chooses to place the point of the arrow, then he is using a space-picture. Essentially there is little difference.

It is convenient for an archer using this method of aiming to shift his anchor-point from under the chin to a point nearer the aiming eye, so that he can look more directly along the shaft. Where this anchor-point is to be is a matter of personal preference, but it must be unchanging and easily recognisable. In this case it is better called a reference point since it may not provide quite the same firmness of contact that the under-chin anchor may provide. I recommend the corner of the mouth, which is sufficiently sensitive. Either the first or second finger can be drawn to this point consistently. It is, however, slightly to the right-hand side of the face, so it is also advisable to lean the head over the shaft very slightly so that the line of vision is directly over the shaft. (Plate 8.) Now if the archer draws to the corner of the mouth while looking steadfastly at the target, he will also be able to see the line of the arrow pointing towards the target a little below eye-level. This will take care of lateral aim. If the arrow persistently goes to the left or right, make sure your aiming eye is vertically above the arrow by lining the bow-string along the arrow.

For vertical aim, you will need to experiment to find out at what distance the arrow-pile is to be placed directly on the centre of the target. To do this you will need plenty of clear open space. Then shoot at 40 yards, say, with your light practice bow and see whether the arrows go high or low, and by moving further away or nearer to the target discover your 'point-on' distance with that bow and those arrows. It will be as well to have plenty of over-shot since you may possibly forget to use the higher reference point. An under-chin anchor-point will naturally send the arrows a lot further. The point-on distance will vary from archer to archer according to the power of the bow, the weight of the arrows, and the reference point used, but if the technique is good, great accuracy can be attained. By further experiment you will be able to estimate just how much higher or lower you should place the point to enable you to hit the target at all ranges.

Some archers get the arrow to lie even closer to the line of sight by placing the three fingers of the drawing-hand underneath the arrow. This is very effective with more powerful bows.

From reading the above, the astute archer will realise it would be possible to shoot point-on at all distances if the fingers were shifted to different points on the string. This is in fact the case. The technique is known as 'string-walking' and is frowned on by purists. Another dodge is to keep the same finger-hold on the string, but to use different reference points on the face according to distance. This, too, is considered unethical. Both methods are forbidden barebow by F.I.T.A. and G.N.A.S. There are even archers who deplore the use of point of aim and the space-picture in that the process is too mechanical and deliberate. These are the true instinctive archers.

Shooting Instinctively

Here the archer attempts to ignore completely the space-picture formed by the arrow and the target. He looks, usually with both eyes open, steadfastly at the target, not deliberately estimating how many yards away it is, but unconsciously getting ready to align himself to that target he sees before him. He will usually draw and loose with a high action fairly quickly because the pose he was going to assume was already in his mind on looking at the target in the first place. Indeed you might say the body assumed the posture required instinctively. It is much like a fielder returning a ball to the wicket. The height, power and flight of the throw are co-ordinated unconsciously. So it is with truly instinctive archery.

Obviously this can be learnt only by constant practice, and practice with the same bow and arrows, for the archer and his tackle must work in co-ordination. His alignment to the target will be governed not only by his subconscious judgement of the distance, but also by his inbuilt knowledge of the performance of his bow. Give him a weaker bow and he will still feel right for elevation while in a position suited to the more powerful bow he is used to–until he has had time to adjust, that is.

Don't be misled into thinking that this is a random method of shooting. The performance of the best instinctive archers would soon disabuse you of that idea. The technique must be just as consistent as in any other form of archery. The training in shooting, though, should be done always at unmarked distances, preferably one shot only from each station, for if many shots are taken from one stand it is virtually impossible to ignore the space-picture. The archer will then begin to calculate and his instinctive ability will be reduced. That is why of four shots made by an instinctive archer from one position, the first shots may well be better than the last. There are rounds, of course, where the archer does have to shoot four shots from one post and at marked distances at that. Even so, the more he can discipline himself to treat each shot as a fresh challenge, the better.

How to Shoot Clout

Since the object of Clout archery is to drop the arrows into a target area at long range (as much as 200 yards for men) a high elevation is required. This necessitates a few minor changes from target basic, though the essentials remain the same. One method may be called conventional, since it retains the usual anchor-point under the chin; the other involves the use of a 'kisser' or attachment to the string drawn to the lips.

To practise either of these methods you must pay particular attention to safety. A highly efficient composite bow could send a target arrow well over 200 yards, even 250 yards. Distances over 330 yards have been achieved by the use of skilled technique. Therefore I suggest you learn the methods first by using a light solid fibre-glass practice bow, say 29 lbs at 28 ins. This is unlikely to send an arrow more than 180 yards, probably considerably less.

Next choose a quiet windless day and find a deserted field over 200 yards long with short grass. Set up a light-coloured flag about 18 ins. square to serve as an aiming mark, at least 50 yards from one end of the field (preferably the north to avoid shooting into the sun), and at least 50 yards from each side. Retire 160 yards from the flag to the other end of the field and take up the normal target archer's stance, but with the feet placed about a foot wider apart for the sake of preserving balance during the shot. Nock, draw and anchor in the usual way, bringing the pile of the arrow on to the marker flag by tilting back from the hips. Continue this movement until the arrow is inclined at about 45 degrees to the ground, no higher. In doing so, pay particular attention to these four points:

(a)   Do not draw any extra length of arrow, or you will be in danger of drawing the shaft inside the bow, causing damage to the arrow and risk of injury to yourself.

(b)   Do not over-extend the bow arm, or you will be likely to hit it with the string and spoil the shot.

(c)   Do not twist the body but lean the upper part of the body from the hips away from the target direction in a true vertical plane. If not, your arrow will fly very wide of the mark. It is because you are liable to do this at first that ample space is needed left and right of the flag.

(d)   Do not elevate the bow arm except by tilting at the hips or you will destroy the correct full-draw position that you learnt in target archery.

At this early stage you will find the assistance of a friend valuable to tell you when you have reached 45 degrees or thereabouts. For safety reasons he should stand at least one yard behind where the shooting line would be.

When you reach 45 degrees, pause and loose neatly and correctly. You may see the arrow during the early part of its flight, then it may disappear at the top of its flight only to come into view again as a streak dropping down towards the area of the flag—maybe a long way to the left or right if you have not tilted and loosed correctly. But if all has been performed accurately, the arrow should fly fairly true for line.

It will in all probability fall slightly short of the flag, but it may reach it, or even go slightly beyond, for the distance reached depends so much on the efficiency of the bow, the weight of the arrow and the style of fletching, the draw-length of the archer, his loosing technique, and the actual elevation at which he shot.

Practise this until the arrows are starting to fall in about a 30 foot group or better, and until you can dispense with the aid of your assistant. The distance you have now reached is the maximum at which you can shoot at a clout target with that bow, those arrows and that technique. If you elevated the arrow less, it would fly low and drop short; if you elevated it more, it would go higher up into the sky but still drop short.

So move the flag and set it in the middle of the group, and see how you fare when you shoot again. You may have to aim off a little for there are wind-currents up aloft that are not discernible at ground level, and anyway your technique may not yet be perfect.

So far so good, but you have yet to learn to aim accurately on to the target. Make a mark in crayon on the lower limb of the bow, corresponding to where the flag appears to be when the bow is at the 45 degree elevation. Get a piece of tape or foam draught-stopper about a foot long and stick it on to the left-hand side of the lower limb between the mark you have made and the lower part of the bow-handle. Insert a sighting pin about 6 ins. above the mark, yes 6 ins. nearer the bow-handle because of the oblique angle at which you will be looking past the lower limb when aiming. Step up 10 yards nearer the target flag and shoot again in the same way as before but aligning the bead on the target flag. This will lower your elevation, but not by as much as you might suppose. If you find the arrows have gone too far, raise the pin by an inch or so (small alterations at this range make little difference). If the arrows have fallen short, lower the pin, but do not go beyond that maximum distance mark you made.

I might digress here and explain that if your bow can shoot further than the flag, then you could have two aiming marks, one above the maximum range mark and one below, but to use the latter would be inadvisable

    (a)   because it is difficult to see at such an extreme angle,

    (b)   because the arrows are sent up sc high that they are in the air longer and travel further, so that errors are magnified.

From the above exercise you will see how to use a sight in Clout shooting with fair accuracy and a conventional method and alter it for different distances within the range of your bow. This method is most suitable for a bow used near the limit of its maximum range. (Plate 9.)

Alternative Method (Using a kisser)

In the method just explained, we increased the distance the arrow could

Plate 9. Aiming at the Clout. Sight on lower limb.

be shot by raising the pile of the arrow while leaving the nock where it was–under the chin. We can achieve the same result by lowering the nock of the arrow without raising the pile above eye-level.

To do this, take your light practice bow and get a friend to mark with indelible pencil the point on the string your lips contact when at full draw in the normal target archery position. Prepare a strip of adhesive tape (zinc oxide plaster will do) about 7 ins. long, 1 cm. wide at one end and tapering to a point at the other. Apply the square end to the string about $4\frac{1}{2}$ ins. above the original mark made and roll the rest of the strip tightly round on itself to form a kind of rounded disc.

Now set the sight pin on the target archery track about 1 in. above the

Plate 10. Aiming at the Clout. Use of kisser.

ledge on which the arrow rests. Put up your flag about 120 yards away and nock and draw in the usual way, but drawing the kisser you have made to touch the lips, endeavouring to preserve your normal draw-length. Do not lean back or tilt the head, and take care to draw the kisser to the lips and the string firmly to the chin. Do not put the lips forward on to the string. The string hand will therefore be drawn to a much lower position than normally and the arrow will fly further than normal when the sight pin is placed on the target flag. (Plate 10.)

To increase the range, move the kisser up the string; to reduce the range, move it down. Being adhesive, it will not move very easily, but it must be secured with whipping once you are satisfied with its position.

It would be disastrous to your scores if it moved during a competition. You will find that to use a kisser placed much higher up the string than 5 ins. from the normal lip position that you had marked for you, will oblige you to use a drawing position so tiring as to be impracticable, but placed in a convenient position it makes accurate shooting possible at longer ranges provided that you are strong enough to maintain an even draw-length and hold steady. It follows, then, that ladies and juniors find the method difficult, but that men are able to use it.

With your light practice bow you will find you cannot comfortably shoot at ranges much over 120 yards with this method, though you should get a tight group. But the users of high efficiency composite bows are enabled to shoot accurately at 160 or 180 yards, which are distances well within the range of their bows. If they attempted to use the conventional method they would find that the sight pin on the lower limb would be so near the underside of the bow-hand as to be impossible to use. It would often need to be placed in the actual position occupied by the bow-hand itself.

Alternative method (with cheek anchor)

If you should find that your sight pin does need to be in a position where your bow-hand obscures it, you could try the field archer's cheek anchor. This will place the arrow nock higher on the face, so that the pin can be placed correspondingly lower on the lower bow limb in a position that may be much more convenient.

If you have learnt any of these methods with the practice bow, and wish to try them with a more efficient bow, do remember that it will have a much greater range. Therefore you will need to practise in a far larger field. You might shoot an arrow over 300 yards, or swing off 50 yards, so be careful in allowing for mistakes and wind-drift.

Chapter 6

Choosing your own equipment

After the initial period of training has passed, the time inevitably comes when the archer wishes either to buy his own equipment or to buy better equipment than he has so far been using. Definite advice can be given only by an experienced archer or coach to a particular archer whom he has watched shooting, but the following general observations may be found useful.

Second-hand Tackle

It is quite likely that a newcomer to archery will be offered tackle by someone who is changing his tackle or leaving the sport. If the price is right, if the tackle is certified to be in good condition by someone qualified to judge, and if the equipment is in every respect identical with what the new archer requires, there is no reason why second-hand tackle should not be bought. But it is this last condition that must be kept well in mind – is it exactly what the archer requires? If not, then he must buy new.

Bows

Most people, after a period with a practice bow, find that its perform-ance is not so good at the longer ranges as the more sophisticated composite bows that other club members may be using, and naturally wish to have one of these. They are tempted to buy one such as is used by, say, the club champion, or are baffled by the multiplicity of bows advertised at a wide range of prices in the catalogues. But the archer should consider the following factors before undertaking what will be a major expense.

Draw-length

The bow must be capable of being drawn to the length of arrow that the archer is going to use. If it is drawn further than intended it is liable to break. But what of the bow that is used below its stated draw-length? Well, the underdrawn bow loses efficiency at the rate of about $1\frac{1}{2}$ to 2 lbs per inch underdrawn, so it is inadvisable to use a bow underdrawn by more than two inches, since the limbs will not have a chance to perform to anything like their full efficiency. Juniors, however, will have to consider the likelihood of their growing during the time that they expect to have the use of the bow.

Length of Bow

To some extent the draw-length of the bow is related to its overall length, but considerable variation in the length of the bow can be made by modifications in the length of the handle section. Many bows today have long handle sections and relatively short working limbs. Other things being equal, a long bow will be more stable than a short bow, and weight for weight will feel easier to control, but it will not have the same cast, i.e. it will not deliver the arrow so fast.

Then, again, one must consider the conditions under which the bow is to be used. A shortish fast bow is desirable for hunting or field archery where undergrowth and obstructions may have to be negotiated. But if a very short bow is drawn to its limit, the angle of the string against the fingers is more acute and this may cause the fingers to slide together and pinch the arrow.

An archer who is not very tall and who uses a short arrow will need a short bow with short fast limbs. An archer who is tall and not particularly strong will require a bow with a longish handle and moderately fast limbs. The average archer must accept a compromise: too long a bow will not give him the range he requires; too short a bow may not be easy to handle confidently, but it should not be difficult to find a bow that will give him a good mark at 100 yards and yet be steady and sweet-shooting.

Draw-weight

This is a ticklish one on which to give advice, for physical strength varies enormously and so does the control of that strength—its co-ordination. A formula which will give the TOP weight a man novice is likely to be able to use is as follows: $1.5 \times$ arrow length in inches = maximum draw-weight in lbs. This would mean that a man drawing a 27 in. arrow is not advised to use a bow more than 40/41 lb at 28 ins., unless he is exceptionally strong. In all probability the average man of this draw-length will be suited with a 38 lb bow. The factor for ladies' bow weight is 1.2, and for juniors under 14 it is 1. Very experienced archers can use heavier weights.

If one can actually have the opportunity of handling a bow of the type and weight under consideration, a better judgement can be made. Do not think, though, that because you can draw a bow three or four times in a shop that you would necessarily be able to loose it cleanly, or shoot a tournament round with it satisfactorily. Some firms, happily, enable the prospective purchaser to shoot the bow on their premises.

You might, it is true, be able to increase your strength by weight-training, or exercises, but the efficient handling of a bow is more a matter of control and technique than of sheer strength. You might think you could gain strength and control just by habitually using the bow, but in my experience this is a mistaken idea. The use of a much heavier bow just for the exercise without loosing it would certainly develop the right muscles, but would not help with the all-important moment of truth – the loose itself. If you shot frequently in a very heavy bow with the idea that you could then use a lighter one more efficiently, you would very likely find your loose deteriorate.

This brings us to the inadvisability of getting a bow that is too much below your strength. Many experienced archers claim that it makes for a poor loose, and while I am not entirely convinced of this, the weight of opinion must be given due consideration. The truth of the matter is, I believe, that an archer can get away with faults in his loosing technique with a heavy bow that would show up more with a lighter bow.

All in all, then, you should get a bow within your strength, heavy enough to give you a good mark at your longest ranges and the flattest trajectory commensurate with your ability to control your shooting throughout a day-long shoot.

Weight-in-hand

This is the actual physical weight of the bow. The heavier the object you hold in your hand the less likely you are to jerk it aside inadvertently, but if it is too heavy you will tire. It is true that the physical weight of the bow is not noticed when at full draw, but the weight is there all the time and must eventually make its presence felt, particularly at the moment of loose, or towards the end of a long shoot. Weight can be built into the bow by the use of heavy woods in the handle section, or metal handle sections, or added afterwards by mercury injection or by weights. Stabilisers and pokers, although they have another function as well, can add to this effect.

It could be argued that if the archer's technique is perfect, the bow will not be diverted from its true position while being shot. This is true, but then whose technique is perfect all the time? It seems to be borne out by recent experience that a fair amount of weight-in-hand is desirable, but it must not be excessive.

Stabilisers

These are projections of metal or similar material in front of or to the side of the bow handle section. They are intended to reduce torque or twisting action of the bow on loose. Even if the hand is placed correctly on the bow there is always a tendency for it to twist slightly since the string does not come away from the fingers in a straight line, no matter how sharp the loose may seem to be. This has been proved beyond all doubt by high-speed photography. An up-and-down movement of the bow may occur, too, but this is usually due to an incorrect pressure on the bow-handle or incorrect loosing technique. Just where such stabilisers should be placed depends a great deal on the archer's technique.

It has been said that stabilisers stabilise the archer rather than the bow, but whatever the truth of the matter, many top-class archers have found that their use has improved their scores.

Design

The actual conformation of the bow limbs is a very technical matter, too involved to be gone into in detail here. The curvature of the limbs, their taper both in width and thickness, all have their effect, and are subject to continual research. So, too, is the material of which they are made. Carbon fibres have been adapted to bow-limb construction. Their lightness and high tensile properties give an increased performance over fibre-glass.

Most composite bows have a working recurve – that is to say, the ends of the limbs are curved forwards and flex when drawn and released, the string being retained in a groove cut into the belly side of the bow. This gives ease of drawing the bow, particularly over the last few inches, coupled with increased cast. Massive recurves produce a very fast cast, hence they are often used in hunting bows, but for target bows a less recurved shape is found preferable.

Handle Shape

It is here that the greatest variety can be seen in bows offered for sale. Some designs are influenced by fashion and appearance only and this is not to be ignored by any means. Laminations of different woods in the handle not only add to the appearance, but also strengthen the handle, since the grain of the different woods can be laid in different directions so as to render warping impossible.

The actual shape of the hand-hold is important, too, since it will dictate the hold to be applied. If you prefer a dropped wrist, a straight wrist or a high wrist when holding the bow, then you should get a bow handle designed to provide whichever you prefer. You cannot expect a bow to perform as the maker intended if you try to hold it in an unsuitable way. Pistol-grips are good in that the wrist is put into its strongest and most uniform position, but the important thing is that you should find it comfortable and consistent.

Cut-out

The important feature here is that the cut-out, which allows the arrow to lie in a near centre-shot position, should extend far enough to enable the archer using the bow to see his sight even at the shortest ranges. A target archer may wish sometimes to shoot at 20 yards indoors; a freestyle field archer may need to sight at even closer ranges. Therefore the sight-window must be at least 1 in. longer than the archer's eye-to-chin measurement, for one must not forget that the arrow is drawn a finger's breadth under the chin. Of course, if an archer is going to use his bow exclusively for barebow shooting with a high anchor the depth of the cut-out is not critical.

Sights

There are so many sights on the market that only general principles can be stated. First, one may use only those permitted under the rules. For instance, those incorporating a lens or prism are not allowed.

A sight should permit easy adjustment by fine degrees both laterally and vertically, and be able to be fixed securely in position once the correct mark has been found.

But where should the sight track be fixed? Here we must consider the mechanics of sighting in the bow. The bow-sight is a front sight. In lieu of a back-sight the archer relies on absolute uniformity of anchor

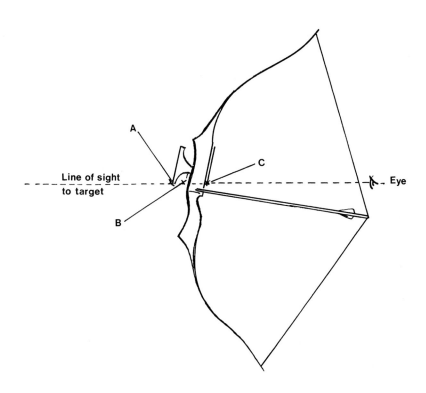

Fig. 3. A sight at A would be hit by the arrow when shot. A sight at B would be grazed by the fletchings. A sight at C would not obstruct either the fletchings or the passage of the arrow.

point, eye-position relative to the arrow, and draw-length. The further away the front-sight is placed, the more accurately he can aim, but this distance will be limited by the flight path of the arrow. Sights that project in front of the bow are excellent at short ranges, but cannot be used at the longest ranges the bow is capable of. If the archer can only just reach his longest distances using a sight, he will be best advised to fix it on the belly side of the bow, otherwise it will be better placed on the back of the bow, that side furthest from him. The diagrams help to make this clear.

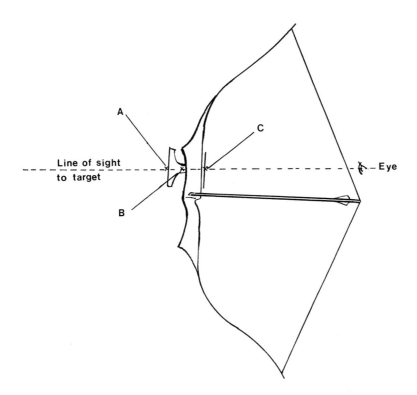

Fig. 4. But at shorter ranges the sight at A or B would be more efficient than a sight at C, because the distance between eye and sight is greater. Moreover, any tendency to torque the bow will more readily become apparent.

Appearance and Finish

This is important, too. There is no reason why an efficient bow should not be attractive to look at – in fact, good looks are often the result of efficiency. As has been said above, the laminations in the handle will add strength where it is needed. The quality of the polish is also of great importance, since the bow is liable to be used in all weathers, and even with care, may sometimes get knocked. A really hard polyurethane finish will help to protect your bow and extend its life and efficiency.

String

Your bow will be provided with a string when you buy it. Be advised, and get a spare of the right size at the same time, rather than waiting until the first one breaks.

Tiller

One last point, examine any bow you buy by looking at it from the side and from both ends after it has been braced. In profile you should see that the limbs are symmetrical, each having the same degree of curvature. But it should be noted here that some bows are deliberately made so that the distance between the lower fade-out and the braced string is perhaps $\frac{1}{4}$ in. less than that between the upper limb fade-out and the string. This is a desirable modification. End on, you should see that the string lies straight down the centre-line of the limbs and that there is no twist, no matter how slight, in the tips of the bow.

Cost

It is unwise to pay too little for a bow so that one later regrets not having paid more for a better article. On the other hand, it is no less discouraging to have paid a high price for a top-quality bow that is found to be unsuitable for the individual using it, though an excellent bow in every other respect.

Arrows
Shaft Material
Arrows can be purchased in all grades of alloy. Some are very soft; others extremely hard. There is no doubt that it is better, if you can afford it, to have the toughest alloy available, for it is essential that

the arrows in a set are all absolutely straight, or consistent shooting is impossible. The best alloy arrows are produced to a carefully controlled specification which may be etched on to the tube. In this way, exact replacements for lost or damaged arrows can be obtained.

What we require in archery are arrows that will flex to suit the bow, but which will not take a permanent set or bend. Arrows made of tubular fibreglass have this quality of never taking a set and of being extremely durable although I have seen some shatter. Up until now there has been a tendency for them to be slightly heavier than alloy shafts and a little more sluggish in their speed of recoil, but this is a drawback which is already being overcome. For the relative beginner, however, alloy shafts are recommended at present.

Length

Once an archer has settled to an established draw-length he has no need of a safety margin and can purchase arrows of the exact length he requires. As has already been explained, he can best determine this by drawing an over-long measuring arrow in the type of bow he intends to use, and getting someone else to take the average of half-a-dozen draws. A fully-drawn arrow will come past the back of the bow but remain on the ledge. There must be no danger of the archer drawing the arrow off the ledge or inside the bow, but any projection of arrow will be so much dead weight. It would also make the use of a clicker or draw-check difficult if not impossible without special attachments.

Spine

The stiffness of the arrow must be matched to the cast of the bow, in order that it may take a path directly to the target aimed at. A well-matched arrow is not deflected off the side of the bow, but snakes round it as shown in the diagram which shows the phenomenon known as The Archer's Paradox.

When the string is released the force of the bow is applied to the nock, which tends to move before the pile, so the shaft bends, and for a variety of reasons it bends inwards. It no longer touches the bow after this but bends round it and eventually takes a course as if it had been shot through the bow. Even if the bow is of centre-shot design the arrow will still flex to some degree. It will be seen, then, that the flexing qualities of the arrow, or spine, must match the cast of the bow. Too stiff an arrow will strike the bow as it passes and fly left (for a right-hander). Too whippy an arrow will not necessarily fly to the right, but it will be erratic. Archery suppliers provide tables which give the recommended spine values for bows of various draw-weights and these are pretty reliable. A good deal depends, though, on the cast of the bow rather than on its draw-weight, and on the archer's loosing technique. It is a good idea to avail oneself of the offer of some suppliers and actually try out a selection of differently spined arrows. All the same, arrow-matching is not quite so critical with the modern composite bow as it used to be with earlier bows because of its centre-shot design.

The dimensions of the tube obviously affect the spine of the arrow, but one can have the same spine with an arrow that has thick walls and a narrow overall diameter as one with thin walls and a wider overall diameter. But the former will be the heavier.

Weight

This is measured in grains. A 28 in. tournament alloy arrow might weigh

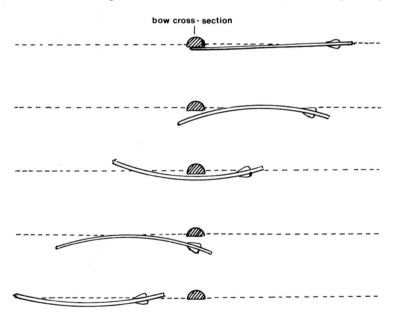

Fig. 5. The Archer's Paradox.

between 250 and 420 grains. Manufacturers' recommendations may be followed or actual experiment undertaken, but the following facts can be borne in mind. A light arrow will be delivered faster but it will slow more quickly, particularly in a head wind, and be more affected by lateral wind-drift. A heavy arrow will not travel so fast initially but will be more stable in flight. A high-efficiency bow will shoot a heavy arrow better than a less efficient bow of the same draw-weight. There is the point, too, that a heavy arrow will stick in the target better than a light arrow because it will have more momentum. Weight of arrow is quite important as spine to provide good performance from the bow.

Cross-sections of two arrows which happen to be of the same spine, i.e. 57 at 27 ins.

(b), being lighter, would have a flatter trajectory than (a), but which would be the more suitable for a given bow would depend on the characteristics of that bow—its draw-weight, for instance.

Again, arrow (c), shown under, would quite likely suit a bow of 36 lbs as well as arrow (b) though its spine is 53 as against 57.

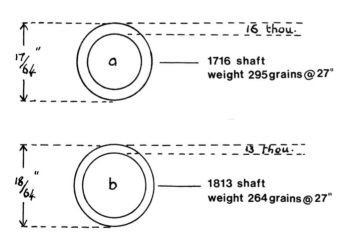

Fig. 6.

Being a great deal heavier, (c) would require a higher trajectory than (b), but might well be preferable provided the archer could get a good mark with it, since it will be less affected by adverse wind conditions. The small difference in spine is unlikely to affect its flight significantly from a centre-shot bow.

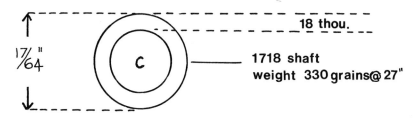

Fig. 7.

The advice then, is to accept the advice of the manufacturers initially, but not to take this as final.

Piles

The pile, which is inserted in the forward end of the shaft, is made either of steel or of alloy. Steel is obviously preferable since it will retain its sharpness better, even after occasionally being shot on to the ground. But generally the steel piles are produced in conical shape (a), and the better-class alloy piles in ogival shape (b).

Some archers claim that (b) gives better penetration than (a), whose angled shoulder tears into the boss, whereas the smooth shape of (b) parts the straw and enables the arrow to slide between.

Advice here is simple. If you use arrows with conical piles and get bouncers, it is possible to grind or file off the sharp shoulder slightly. Take care to remove only a very little, though, or you will damage the arrow. If you use arrows with ogival piles, keep them sharp and try to avoid missing the target through shooting at ranges much beyond your capabilities before you have gained the requisite skill.

Archers using the best quality tournament arrows can now get bullet piles as an alternative to the conical ones, it having been proved that they give better penetration.

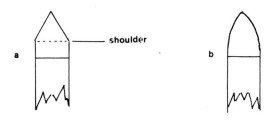

Fig. 8. Types of Pile.

Nocks

Some nocks are inserted into the tube by force-fit; some screw into a threaded socket; some screw on to a tapered thread; and some are glued on to a swaged or tapered end of the tube. Of these the last is the best, because there is less chance of another arrow striking the nock of an arrow in the target and splitting the shaft, rendering it beyond repair. Various materials are used, nylon and a variety of plastics. The essential qualities are that they should be uniform in slot size, should be reason-

Fig. 9. Insert Nock.   Exterior Nock.

ably durable and not prone to spreading or distortion when put on a nocking point of the correct size.

As regards colour, well, this is partly a matter of personal choice, partly a matter of expediency. It is an aid to recognition through binoculars to have brightly fluorescent nocks, but the range of colours is limited, and it is quite likely that you will have someone else on your target with the same coloured nocks at some time or another.

Shapes vary. The bow-hunter may prefer an index nock which has a ridge in line with the cock feather which enables him to nock an arrow correctly without taking his eyes from the quarry, but this is no advantage to the target archer who has plenty of time to select and nock his arrow.

Provided the slot is well-shaped and deep enough to secure the arrow on the string, and the outer shape so designed as to reduce the likelihood of pinching, one can please oneself.

Snap-on nocks which actually clip on to the string are good in that they are less likely to be pushed off by accident while the arrow is being drawn, and in that they allow the string to rotate in the nock without dislodging the arrow, but care must be taken to ensure that all the arrows in the set can be shot and released with the same degree of freedom and that the nocking point is arranged so that the nock cannot accidentally be moved up and down the string.

Fletching

This is the most important part of the arrow assembly since a badly-fletched arrow cannot fly true.

One should observe when purchasing that feather fletchings are all of the same quality and stiffness, that they are all set on straight, or off-set at the same angle. Owing to the characteristics of feathers, even straight-fletched arrows will rotate in flight. This is why it is important that all the fletchings on an arrow must be taken from the same 'wing', either all left-wing or all right-wing, for the primary feathers on the left wing of a bird grow in the reverse shape from those on the right wing. So if mixed left- and right-wing fletchings were used on the same arrow they would induce contrary rotations causing the arrow to 'flirt' or fly erratically. It is very unlikely that you would get incorrectly fletched arrows from any competent manufacturer, but matching of fletchings is a point to remember when you are repairing or refletching your own arrows. This natural rotation of the shaft when feathers are used can be increased either by off-setting the fletchings (setting them at an angle), or by spiral fletching. A modest amount of off-set, say 2 degrees, will give satisfactory rotation to hold the arrow on its course and yet not cause it to lose speed too rapidly. It is important that the underside of the fletchings face the pile of the arrow.

Plastic fletchings, being man-made, are more likely to be uniform than feather fletchings, but they are more easily dislodged and damaged by accidental knocks, and are therefore not recommended for beginners. For advanced archers, though, they are preferable. For one thing, they are not affected by wet weather as feather fletchings are.

Next, number of fletchings. Should one use three- or four-fletched arrows? Well, for an arrow to be held on course a certain minimum area of fletching is necessary. Consequently, each of the fletchings on a four-fletch arrow can be smaller than each of those on a three-fletch arrow, reducing the effect of a cross-wind. Other than that, as I see it, there is little advantage. Since three-fletch will be cheaper, the relative beginner is advised to use these.

Surprisingly enough, the actual shape seemes to be of much less importance than the area of fletching, but it is advisable not to have fletchings that stand very high from the shaft, or they are likely to get damaged or affect the arrow as it passes the bow.

Colour is to be considered, too. Even though arrows will be crested and named, it is a help to recognition when taking scores if your fletchings are of a distinctive colour. Even more important is your ability to recognise them in a target, with binoculars if need be, from the shooting line, so that errors can be rectified without delay, which could seriously affect your score. Fluorescent plastic fletchings show up well, but as has been explained in connection with nocks, there is only a narrow range of colours available. A Field Archer shooting a Hunter's Round on a virtually all-black target face will benefit from using light-coloured fletchings, unless he is in the habit of placing them all in the white spot, of course! Without being unduly pessimistic, there is also the possibility of archers, target or field, having to look for arrows in the grass. Green fletchings and cresting are obviously an unwise choice from this point of view, and in some summers yellow will not be very noticeable, either. Red and orange sound very distinctive colours, and so they are, but that is why so many archers use them!

Price

The archer is offered arrows at a very wide range of prices. If he has just passed the beginner's stage he will want something better than the very cheapest and endeavour to get a reasonable match to his bow without running to the heavy expense of the very best arrows money can buy. It is doubtful whether he will have the skill to benefit from the fine quality of the best arrows and will quite likely do just as well with cheaper ones. Faults will be his own and will not be attributable to variation in individual arrows. Again, the medium-priced arrows are often colour-matched so that although he has no choice of colour he can get replacements very easily by return of post. The beginner is more likely to damage or lose arrows than the experienced archer. Yet, if money were no object, even the beginner would do well to get the best arrows obtainable since he could be absolutely sure that any errors were of his own making, and he would be able to get an exact replacement for any shaft he lost or damaged by quoting the specifications etched on the shaft or printed on the box. If he did not want to delay while his own distinctive colour and style of fletchings were attached, he could buy a fletching jig, with which he could enjoy both the economy and satisfaction of fletching his own shafts.

The beginner at field archery will be far more likely to lose arrows than his target archer counterpart, because of the rough terrain he will shoot over, and probably he will use wooden or cheap alloy arrows at first. It will not be long, however, before he too will benefit from better quality arrows. Although these will be more expensive, he will be less likely to lose them for two reasons. One, they will shoot straighter and suit his bow better; two, they will be less likely to become bent and no longer fly true. In fact, the dedicated field archer will use arrows no less high in quality than the dedicated target archer, unless he prefers to use wooden arrows for the sake of tradition or because he feels they are more appropriate to this style of shooting. But even then, the dedicated field archer will use the best wooden arrows he can make or buy.

Taking everything into account, get the best arrows you can afford; the better archer you are, the more you can benefit from high quality arrows and the accuracy of their matching, one to another, in a set.

Other Items

There is no reason why the same bracer and tab bought initially should not continue to be perfectly satisfactory. The same applies to the ground quiver which was recommended to hold the arrows while the beginner is shooting on the line. But now some other form of quiver will be found useful. At target tournaments ground quivers may be taken on the line, but may not be left there after one has finished shooting. Therefore it is best to keep the ground quiver behind the line as a bow support and a holder for spare arrows, while the archer retains the arrows he is about to use in a belt quiver of some kind. This can easily be home-made and some very fine examples of decorative craftwork may be seen. Whether home-made or bought, though, the quiver should have an efficient design. It should be deep enough to hold the arrows securely, and have space enough for at least six arrows. Moreover, it will be found an advantage to have a means of separating the arrows, so that particular ones may be selected. The archer may choose to shoot them in a numbered order, or to put one or more on one side for some reason.

For field archery, shoulder quivers are often used. The advantage of these is that they can hold a far greater number of arrows to allow for loss or damage while shooting over 14 targets or more, and also have a pocket for a reserve string, a knife and other necessities that a field archer may require. The target archer will be able to keep his spares in his tackle box by his seat behind the line, but the field archer will have to carry his with him. Nevertheless, the shoulder quiver has certain disadvantages for the field archer. One is that arrows carried on the back are liable to catch in overhanging foliage when the archer bends to negotiate an obstacle. Another is that it is easy to spill half-a-dozen arrows when one bends down to retrieve or search for arrows in the ground. Again, it is not always easy to select the particular arrow you require when the nocks are bunched just behind your right ear. A much more convenient design for the field archer is the holster quiver in which a fair number of arrows may be carried, sloping backwards. Here they are readily available, can be selected easily and do not catch in undergrowth as one passes through. Such a quiver is perfectly suitable for target archery also. It will usually include a pocket for spare strings and other necessities, a retainer for a pencil and a clip to hold score cards. A tassel is a useful addition as its function is to dry and clean arrows.

Clothing

Advice has already been given to the archer to wear clothing that will not obstruct his shooting. Now we must consider other aspects – such as colour. For important British and F.I.T.A. meetings certain standards of dress are insisted upon and it seems likely that the tendency will be to extend this practice to minor meetings also. For information on this the reader is referred to the G.N.A.S. Rule Book, where he will read, among other things, that plain dark green and/or white are the recommended colours in British events. Indeed at a target meeting, some uniformity of colour and dress is desirable and enhances the sense of occasion, without preventing some individuality being exercised.

In field archery, however, the widest imaginable range of attire may be seen. For one thing the archers are not assembled together at one time except at the beginning and end of the shoot; for another, field archers like to express their individuality more than target archers although there may be a good case for the members of a team to adopt a common uniform if they wish. As regards colour, there is one very good reason for choosing bright colours–safety. A good field course is laid out with safety very much in mind, but because small groups are shooting in succession around a course often in wooded or rough country, it is a desirable practice to wear clothes than can be readily distinguished from the background. Again, because of the rougher country, women will find slacks or trousers far preferable to skirts for field archery, no matter what the practice may be for target archers.

Another point to be borne in mind is that of the weather. Shooting often has to continue in cold or wet weather and suitable clothing will need to be worn that will give protection without adversely affecting the archer's shooting.

While we are considering clothing we might as well consider footwear too. This should be serviceable and comfortable. Waterproof footwear may be needed on occasions. Women will need to remember that it is not possible to be steady in high heels, particularly on soft ground, and that to change from high heels to low heels in the course of shooting would very likely affect the stance.

By now, it will be seen that the archer is accustomed to carry a good deal of gear to a shoot and so it is advisable to keep this in a tackle box for convenient transportation. The bow, too, should be kept in a bow case to protect it from the weather and from chance knocks.

A repair outfit will be found useful. At first only a few obvious necessities, like beeswax, nocking thread, glue and spare nocks will be carried, but it is amazing how items that might come useful accumulate, until one needs a sizeable tool-box to accommodate them all.

Other equipment that may be seen at tournaments may not be essential, but it is certainly useful. This may include a folding chair, an umbrella or a small tent to shelter under in wet weather in the intervals between shooting, and a small 'scratcher', or one-pronged rake for unearthing lost arrows, alas, too often necessary. For target shooting and marked distance field archery, many archers use binoculars or monoculars to spot their arrows. A good degree of magnification is necessary, but this is not the only factor to be considered. There is also the brightness of the image, which is why there should be a good ratio of magnification to the diameter of the objective lenses. Binoculars of the specification 7×50 will give good results. Those providing magnifications of 12 times or more are difficult to hold steady and are therefore not advised.

There is little doubt that in spite of this list being fairly exhaustive, you will in time find yet other equipment useful, but do not neglect to consider the possibility of theft or loss. Tackle has been known to disappear from cars, whether locked or unlocked, from club huts that were thought to be secure, and all too often from roof racks when it has not been strapped on. Insurance cover may not restore the goods, but it certainly eases the blow when such accidents occur.

Chapter 7

Improving Your Shooting

How in fact do archers attempt to improve their shooting? The following are some of the ways, described in the order in which they occur to most archers:
1. By buying new tackle.
2. By copying an expert.
3. By shooting haphazardly as often as possible.
4. By reading the available literature.
5. By going to a coach.
6. By analysing their own technique.
Let us examine these in detail.

1. Buying New Tackle

It will be evident from the previous chapter that if an archer has been using unsuitable equipment, he will benefit from changing it to something more suitable. He may have been using a bow so heavy that he can neither control it nor hold it steady and has therefore succumbed to the temptation to snap-shoot. His arrows may have been too short so that he has been obliged to adopt a crouching posture preventing the shoulders from opening out to a comfortable extent. His arrows may not have been matched to the bow and may not have performed consistently. His tab or glove may have been clumsy or ill-shaped, causing erratic loosing.

Nevertheless, indiscriminate changing of tackle rarely brings lasting success. At first some improvement may be found, but this is often due to the spell of increased confidence which allows the archer to shoot in a more relaxed way with beneficial results. The time will come when he is back where he was before.

The same comment applies to the use of gimmicks or devices that do not contravene the rules, and which, it is hoped, could lead to better scores.

But the best and most permanent way of acquiring better scores is to improve the shooting technique itself, which means becoming more consistent. The use of a gimmick with a bad style will not bring lasting benefit.

All the same, the ambitious archer is advised to consider his tackle and to get the best – that which is most suitable for him.

2. Copying an Expert

This is generally inadvisable. It is a fallacy to suppose that if you copied every detail of an individual expert's shooting that you would shoot as well: you might not be built the same. Again, it is a fact that some high-scoring archers use very peculiar styles. Who knows, they might have shot better still had they learnt a more orthodox style.

But no one, in fact, ever does copy another's style in every detail. There are always some aspects liable to be overlooked by the observer, and if you copy only part of the style, you will not get the same results. It may well be that the expert you choose to copy has compensating faults. Where will you be if you copy only part of his style?

3. Frequent Shooting

On the face of it, this sounds excellent advice, but it should be 'considered' shooting. To shoot as often as possible for the sake of the scores alone is not a good idea. Constant practice is sound, but let it *be* practice. A few dozen arrows shot with careful consideration, for the sake of ironing out some known inconsistency, will do far more good than hurrying through a round so as to turn in yet another score card. Of course, you feel fine when you put up a score better than you have achieved before, but then you become despondent when you fail to maintain the improvement. High scores come as the result of good shooting, but to consider scores alone as the basis of improvement is a barren pursuit.

4. Reading about it

The enthusiastic archer will read all he can about the sport and about the techniques advised by various writers, but these do not always tally. He must have some yardstick by which to test the reliability of the advice given. You may say he can do this by trying the techniques himself; but too many archers spend so much time experimenting that they develop no consistent style of their own. Then, again, one must give a new method a fair test. Frequently an archer tries a new idea for five minutes, then discards it, forgetting he has spent perhaps five years shooting in his original way. But it is a good thing to read widely and to keep an open mind. One might do a lot worse than to re-read 'Toxophilus' by Roger Ascham, the first book in English on the subject of archery!

5. *Going to a Coach*

This will undoubtedly be of benefit, for a good coach will not try to force you into some standardised style that he prefers, but will endeavour to diagnose what is wrong with your shooting by observing inconsistencies and by advising you how best to overcome them. It is likely that he will be able to detect faults you were unaware of yourself. But you must put your trust in him and he must have time to put you right. Some faults can be rectified almost at once; others may be ingrained after years of bad habit. The latter may require several sessions to eradicate. A full week-end's concentrated work may be needed to effect a major improvement. Moreover, a clear understanding must be achieved of what is to be done. It is no use going away from a coaching session only to relapse into the old bad habits. Some archers expect a magic formula to be confided to them that will ensure better scores, but are unwilling to undertake the hard graft that may be needed.

Still, if you go to a coach and ask for advice, you have taken a valuable first step towards improvement, because without your co-operation he cannot assist you. That is why most coaches do not offer advice unasked even when they see it would be useful—they wait for the approach to be made by the archer. So far, practically all G.N.A.S. coaches have been amateur and so their time is limited not only by the need to earn a living, but also by the modest demands of their own shooting, so you may not be able to get a coach's assistance when you want it. Accordingly, the following advice is given, on much the same lines as would be given by a coach. Do not, though, use it as some misguided people use a 'Home Doctor' and imagine you suffer from every ailment that is treated here.

6. *Analysing Your Own Shooting*

To improve your own shooting, you must first analyse what's wrong with it. There may be several things wrong. In this case do not try to put everything right at once, but deal with one thing at a time, so that you can concentrate on it and avoid drawing false conclusions. Some errors are fundamental and lead to others, so deal with these first. Generally deal with your faults in the order in which they occur in the sequence of shooting. For instance, an incorrect positioning of the fingers on the string may lead to an unduly high elbow and this to a dropping of the bow-arm on loose. In this case it would be useless to attempt to cure the dropping of the bow-arm before attending to the placing of the fingers on the string.

If you are a relative beginner you will do well to keep fairly closely to the techniques detailed in Chapters 4 and 5. But if you have been taught by another method or have been shooting for some time, you will have introduced variations. This is not necessarily a bad thing – the Basic Method is what it says, basic – individuals will adapt the method to their own requirements. But you need to be sure that the variations you have brought in are beneficial. So check again step by step to see in what respects you have moved away from Basic. You may find that a return to the original procedures is advisable. If you are convinced, however, that some of your individual methods are consistent, then they are good, too, and there is no reason why you should not continue with them. Remember: there is only one requirement for good shooting – to do the same thing in the same way every time.

It is always useful to look at the pattern made by arrows in the target, but one must beware against drawing hasty conclusions, since there may be a variety of reasons for an arrow flying in a given direction. Errors in the vertical plane are due to one set of causes, those in the horizontal plane to another set, while a combination of both will cause a scatter on the target. It is up to you to identify the cause in your particular case and since it is your equipment itself which may be at fault, you should first make sure that this is in good order.

Check on Tackle

1. The string must have a suitable number of strands so as to give consistent performance.
2. The centre-servings and nock-servings must be secure with no frayed or broken strands in evidence.
3. The bow must be braced to the right bracing-height, according to the maker's specifications, or to your own experience of the

bow. A useful guide is to observe that there is about ½ in. of string-groove showing when the bow is braced.

4. The nocking-point should be built up sufficiently to hold the arrow nock, but not too tightly, and it should be set at about ⅛ in. above the right-angle.

5. The arrow must be secure and the 'finger' of some types not worn away or weakened.

6. The fletchings must be in sound condition, the nocks of the same dimensions and the arrow shafts straight. An ancient test that is still worth applying is to balance the shaft horizontally on the thumb- and finger-nails of one hand. If it is then spun sharply, a straight shaft will remain on the nails, while a bent one will leap off.

7. The arrows should be of a suitable spine. If they have been supplied matched to the bow by a reputable supplier it will be possible to shoot them well. Many peculiarities in the behaviour of arrows are traceable to faults of technique. The modern composite bow will accept arrows of a wider range of spine values than is generally realised.

8. Plastic fletchings, if used, must clear the bow. Failure to do so is not easy to detect, but one can often hear the slap, may see the erratic behaviour of the arrow, and may find vanes damaged in a compatible way – there may be marks also on the bow or rest.

9. The bracer must be correctly placed and the tab in good condition, smooth and trimmed to shape.

10. The sight-track should be vertical and the slide not liable to slip. The sight-pin should not be excessively extended.

If all these things are in order, it is a fair assumption that errors on the target reflect errors in your technique. The pattern you obtain in the target will in all probability be one of the following: a group, a scatter, a vertical line or a horizontal line.

A Group

If you consistently get a tight group at 20 yards or 30 metres, say, that can be covered by the palm of your hand, there is not much wrong, though it can still be improved. If the group is not in the centre of the target it is tempting to move the sight in the direction of the error as indicated in Chapter Four, and often this will give satisfactory results, but an excessive amount of sight-pin, for example, could cause trouble at change of distances, for bow-cant or anchor-point at side of face could be the cause.

A Scatter

This will show that a number of faults are present in your shooting, each of which has caused its own effect.

A Vertical Line

Most vertical, or near vertical, errors are caused by faults in the D.F.L. (Draw Force Line, see fig. 10), or draw length and loose. Before examining technique let us examine possible causes of vertical errors connected with the tackle which will make it clear why this should be checked before conclusions are drawn:

1. The sight may have slid up or down the track.
2. A kisser, if used, may have slipped.
3. Arrows may be bent.
4. The tab may have been recently powdered, causing a sharper loose, or allowed to get worn and dull. The best plan is not to powder the tab at all.
5. The centre-serving may have slipped and, with it, the nocking point.
6. The string may have let down, causing alteration in the nocking-point angle.
7. The rest may have become weakened.
8. In rain, the feathers may have become wet and depressed. This may cause the arrows to fly high at short range as the feathers offer less drag. But at long range the arrows may fall short, because the fletchings have not been able to keep the arrow on steady flight and the consequent 'flirt' of the shaft will have caused excessive drag.
9. Nocks may have had variable slot-size, tight ones causing a degree of 'pluck-back'.
10. A head or following wind may have affected the flight. To some extent the effects are obvious, but it should be borne in mind that some archers maintain that a head wind at short range can cause the arrows to fly high.

The possible variations in technique are as follows, the fundamental ones being concerned with D.F.L. and loose:

1.   Variable draw-length. An underdrawn arrow will tend to go low left and one drawn further than normal, high right. This left or right tendency is due to the increase or reduction in effective spine. They go high or low, of course, because of the alteration in cast of the bow.

2.   Variable anchor-point, causing alteration in the inclination of the arrow.

3.   Mouth open, or teeth separated while the lips are closed.

4.   Fingers loosing the string one after another, allowing the bow to swivel to a fresh inclination before the string is finally loosed. If the third finger releases the string first, the shot will tend to go high and vice versa.

5.   String slapping the bracer. This will cause loss of power behind the arrow besides diverting it.

6.   Snatched, forward or dead loose.

7.   Loosing on the move, while the sight is being brought up or down to the mark, particularly if unit-aiming is not practised.

8.   Spasming, or nervous reflex.

9.   Pinching the arrow so that it is lifted off the rest.

10.   Lifting the arrow off the rest with the forefinger of the bow-hand. This is more likely to happen with a practice bow not fitted with a supplementary rest.

11.   Heeling or topping the bow by applying pressure below or above the centre.

12.   Fingers closing on the bow at the moment of loose, causing alteration of its alignment.

13.   Creeping, failing to maintain draw-length. Arrow will tend to go low left.

14.   D.F.L. incorrect, elbow of the shaft-arm being too high or too low.

15.   Locked bow-elbow, unless the bow is free to move.

16.   Inaccurate aiming.

The diagram shows the correct D.F.L., which may be compared with the photograph of the archer on page 37. It will be seen that the elbow of the drawing arm, the nock of the arrow and the pressure point of the hand on the bow are in the same straight line. The arrow is not in line

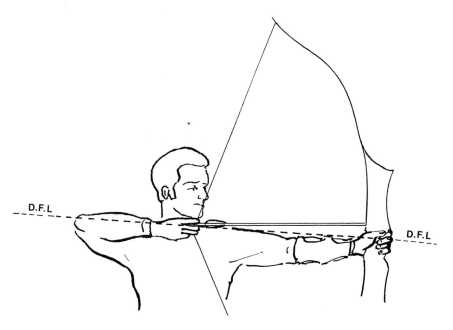

Fig. 10. The Draw-Force Line.

with the forearm of the arm drawing the string and is not intended to be. It is the bow that must be held in balance, not the arrow. Then when the string is released there will be no tendency for the bow to move off the D.F.L. It is essential that the bow be supported at the tiller-point, that point on the handle from which the limbs have been constructed to bend in balanced curves. If the bow-handle has been correctly shaped, this is where the hand will naturally be placed, but guard against 'heeling' the bow. That is, applying pressure below the proper hand-hold – a dropped wrist is very liable to do this. If this is done the bow will tend to tilt upward on loose and the shot go high.

If one shoots with a high drawing elbow, the tendency will be for the bow-arm to drop on loose, causing the arrow to go low. This fault is commonly caused by overloading the forefinger, so make sure the fingers are correctly placed on the string before you begin to draw. Get a good Preparation Line (see page 35) and you are half-way to a good D.F.L. In the Prep-Line the arrow is aligned with the forearm of the drawing arm merely because there is nothing else to relate it to at that stage.

Take a light hold on the bow and leave this unchanged throughout the loose. Gripping the bow tightly will waste effort and make it less steady. A sudden squeeze at the moment of loose will tend to jerk it away from the mark. The bow will behave better if it is supported at the tiller-point and not gripped. This is why some archers use a sling so that they can shoot the arrow without actually holding the bow. This is a good idea as long as you let the sling do the work and do not snap the fingers shut involuntarily.

The middle joints of the fingers and the wrist of the drawing arm must be straight and relaxed, and there should be no tension in the forearm, biceps or chest muscles either, all the weight of the bow being taken across the shoulders. Only the muscles operating the end-joints of the fingers should retain the string. The tip of the forefinger should be touching firmly under the point of the chin. It should not follow the jaw-line. If it does, either the drawing elbow will be raised too high or the wrist will be twisted, both detrimental to good shooting. On loose, the hand and forearm should retreat slightly along the D.F.L., while the bow hand continues to push out along the D.F.L. If the forefinger is not located under the chin, but with a space between it and the chin, then it is obvious that the shot will go high, because the arrow will be tilted up more. Uniformity of placing the finger below the chin, and therefore below the aiming eye, could be achieved by using a 'kisser', or a similar attachment of the string intended to be drawn to the nose, but to my mind this achieves nothing that cannot be achieved more simply, and may introduce other errors. The mouth must be kept shut, too, of course.

The essential features of a good full-draw position are the D.F.L., the upright relaxed position of the head and shoulders and a good extension of the shoulders. The action by which the bow is brought to this position is the draw proper. The one taught to beginners in Chapter 4 is known as the V-draw and is the easiest to learn and teach. Many archers use the T-draw or a modified form of it. In this, the bow is raised and presented vertically to the target before the string is drawn. This means that the shoulders must be moved out of alignment in stage 1 and brought back again in stage 2. Provided this is done and the bow-arm shoulder is not permitted to collapse, the method is sound. Then there is the high draw and modifications of it, whereby the bow is raised above the target before being drawn. Done properly this is quite satisfactory, too, and may be of benefit to paraplegics who will be better able to maintain their balance, and to archers who tend to hunch the bow shoulder with the V-draw.

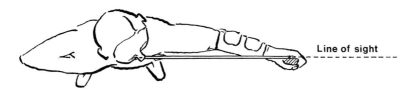

Fig. 11. E.S.A.R.

A Horizontal Line

Most horizontal errors are caused by faults in the E.S.A.R. (Eye, sight, arrow relationship) (Fig. 11). Let us once again check our tackle before analysing technique. Variations can be summarised as follows:

1. Loss of bracing-height, causing the arrow to be directed more to the left at the moment it leaves the string.
2. Plastic fletchings fouling bow.
3. Bent arrows.
4. Arrows slapping bow, being far too stiff; or kicking erratically if far too whippy.
5. Wind drift. The effect of a cross-wind at short ranges is often exaggerated; more often the archer himself or the bow has been moved by the wind.

Possible errors in technique are as follows, the fundamental ones being to do with E.S.A.R.:

1. Creeping. Arrow will go low, but left as well, owing to the effective spine being increased.
2. Locked bow elbow with the bow held tightly.
3. Bent fingers of the string-hand. This will mean that the fingers move away to the right of the face before a real loose is achieved, so the arrow goes left.
4. Fly-away loose, the fingers flung stiffly away from the face, making the arrow go left.
5. Dog-legging the string. By this, I mean imparting a kink into the string by failing to keep the string-hand vertical. This will mean that although the forefinger may be under the chin, the third finger will bring the string to the right, and with it, the arrow nock, causing the shaft to be directed to the left.
6. String slapping bracer.
7. Variable head TURN, causing variation in E.S.A.R. The archer will see more or less bow-window.
8. Variable head ANGLE, causing the same effect.
9. Variable anchor-point. If the anchor-point is consistently to the right of the centre of the chin, the arrows will tend to group left, but there is also the likelihood of alteration of draw-length, which will send the arrows high or low as well.
10. Canting bow. If the top limb is tilted to the right, the arrow will fly left; if to the left, the arrow will fly right.
11. Torquing the bow. If pressure is placed on the right-hand side of the bow-handle, the arrows will tend to fly left, and vice versa.
12. Wind sway on archer. A stable standing position should be established.
13. Spasming, or nervous reflex.
14. Loosing on the move, as the sight is brought across from left to right, or right to left. Unit-aiming will help to reduce this, but one should concentrate on steadying on aim.
15. Incorrect aiming. Closing the wrong eye will cause the arrow to fly a long way left, but this is unlikely to occur except with a beginner. Smaller errors can be caused by carelessness and lack of concentration.

For accurate aiming with a sight it is essential that the aiming eye, the sight pin, the nock of the arrow and the pile of the arrow should be in the same vertical plane. At short ranges the figure so described will be virtually a parallelogram.

If it is tilted or distorted, the arrow cannot go where you are aiming. Now there are various ways in which the E.S.A.R. may be out of true. The head may be tilted so that the eye is not above the arrow nock under the middle of the chin. The head may be correctly turned but the nock drawn slightly to the side of the chin. The head may be correctly turned and the bow canted. Both the head and the bow may be canted. Where these errors are present the arrows may be brought on target by means of altering the sight pin at any one distance, but it will be found that at change of distance, not only will the sight have to be moved up or down the bow, but also the extension of the sight pin will have to be modified. This introduces a fresh variable which is detrimental to accurate shooting. A great extension of the sight pin in quiet weather conditions is a sure sign that something is wrong with the technique, either head angle, loose or hand-hold on the bow, provided the bracing height of the bow is right and the arrows of the right spine. A word here about Barebow shooting in Field style, where both the head and the bow may be canted. The E.S.A.R. is correct here, for the line of vision is directly above the line of the shaft. Since the barebow archer has no sight, he is not concerned with its extension or position and shoots accurately to the mark at which he is looking.

A common fault is for the arrows to fly left for a right-hander, even when the E.S.A.R. seems to be correct and the arrows of the correct spine. Frequently this is due to a twist being imparted into the string by the fingers of the drawing hand, so that at the moment of loose the string is plucked to the right of centre. To avoid this, take care to advance the drawing hand to the face during draw at the same speed that the bow is brought to the vertical, and to ensure that the fingers and back of the drawing hand are flat to the line of the bow at all times. In other words, the back of the drawing hand should be vertical at full draw. It is also necessary that the hand releases the string from its correct position in front of the chin, and does not fly away from the face as it looses the string. The hand should move back close to the neck.

The frustrating fault whereby the arrow falls from the ledge or rest while being drawn is due to this turning of the hand beyond vertical. It is not pinching that causes this so much as the contact of the second finger with the nock of the arrow. It is because the beginner is prone to twist the hand out of line that he is advised to leave a space between the arrow and the second finger, so as to reduce the likelihood of dislodging the shaft.

A check on the correctness of degree of head turn can be applied by lining up the string with the centre-line of the bow–not the sight-pin. A study of the E.S.A.R. diagram will show why this is so. The string, on loose, moves toward the centre-line of the bow, not towards the sight. The centre-line of a right-handed composite bow is probably along the left-hand edge of the cut-out, so it will be near the sight-pin in its normal position but not so close as to obscure it. If you see a 'window', that is, a space between the bow and the string, this is a sure sign that the aiming eye is not vertically above the nock. If the archer is very prone to faulty head angle, then he might well check the lining up of the string every time; otherwise I would advise only an occasional check as it can distract the archer's attention from the mark he is aiming at.

The Loose

This is the most important part of the archer's technique and one should make every effort to perfect it. The string should be loosed positively by all three fingers simultaneously from the full-draw position on the chin. The fingers should release the string when the archer wishes it, but they should not be flung open stiffly. If the fingers are bent at the middle knuckles a considerable amount of finger movement is required in order to release the string, so that in all probability the string will be loosed to the right of the face and the arrow fly left (for a right-hander). If all three fingers do not release the string simultaneously, the bow will begin a tilting movement before the arrow is shot which is impossible to standardise. If the first finger releases the string before the second and third, the bow will tilt downwards. If the third releases the string before the second and first, the bow will tilt upwards. Both of these faults are usually traceable to a faulty position of the elbow, below or above the true D.F.L.

The archer should try to get complete relaxation in the drawing arm, thinking of it as a chain with flexible links drawn by the back muscles. When he is satisfied with the rest of his technique and the aim and is ready to loose, he should apply a little more effort across the shoulders, using the muscles that will draw back the drawing elbow. No movement may be noticeable to an onlooker, but this will apply a slight extra pressure of the string on the chin. If then the fingers loose the string, the drawing hand will move back slightly. It must do so unless you prevent it, for you have let go of a weight of, say, 30 to 40 pounds. If the hand does not move back, you have proof positive that you have needlessly tensed the muscles in the front of the chest and forearm. This movement is important, as without it the string will travel away from the chin before being loosed. Some archers continue the movement of the drawing hand until it is behind the head or further still. There is no harm in this, if the archer is enabled thereby to effect a clean loose, but it is necessary not to start turning the hand before the string has been completely released. If the fingers and wrist are kept relaxed they will show this relaxation immediately after the loose as in the photograph on page 40.

If the arrow is allowed to creep before being loosed, either because of collapse of the bow arm and shoulder or because of the drawing hand moving forward before releasing the string (the forward loose), the effective length of the arrow will be shortened and less effort applied by the bow. For a right-hander this will send the arrow low left–low because of the reduced power, left because the arrow will behave as if it were stiffer as it will not flex so much.

To avoid creeping some archers employ either a visual draw-check or an audible one, a clicker. If the visual draw-check is near the arrow pile, it is necessary to look away from the mark and the sight to observe it. While the eye is being focussed again on the mark, creep may begin to set in again. The clicker has not this disadvantage, but the archer has to loose immediately the click is heard or he has no means of knowing that he is any longer fully drawn. This is considering the clicker purely as an audible draw-check, of course–it has other functions.

Better than using such an aid is training oneself to draw and maintain an even draw length by the physical feel of the action. It can be done, but requires practice. One way of training oneself is to practise blind loosing. For this the archer should go ten yards or so from a blank target, set his sight accordingly, and when he has satisfied himself by a practice shot or two that it is about right, he should draw and aim at the centre of the boss and close the eyes. (It is as well to have the assistance of another archer to observe that all is in order.) While the eyes are closed the archer will feel every detail of his technique without being distracted by any visual impression. He will feel the draw-weight of the bow across the shoulders, the relaxation in the drawing arm, the pressure of the string against the chin, and the cleanness and neatness of the loose. If he is at fault he will notice the absence of these requisites. But it is necessary to spend some time with the eyes closed, say, 3 to 7 seconds, as it is only then that the mechanics of the loose can be concentrated upon. There is no value at all in the exercise if the arrow is loosed immediately the eyes are closed. This exercise will certainly refine the loose. It is also useful to reduce tensions arising from anxiety about aiming.

If having drawn the bow, aimed and closed the eyes for, say, 7 seconds, you open them to find the aim has drifted off, you should adjust your stance accordingly, for you are obviously not standing in the ideal posture to maintain true aim naturally.

Follow-through

Not only should the drawing hand be taken back along the D.F.L.; so also should the bow hand be maintained on the D.F.L. or allowed to move forward along it slightly. If the bow arm is rigidly fully extended and the bow gripped, as soon as the string is loosed the bow will tend to move because the load of 30 to 40 pounds has been let go. Since it cannot move forward, it will swing sideways, the arrow with it. The elbow may be locked and the bow left free to move in a sling, in which case accurate shooting is quite possible, as long as the string clears the bracer.

The Hold

Faulty placing of the hand on the bow-handle can cause arrows to fly left or right. If the wrist is placed too far in the bow, the bow may be torqued in such a way that the arrow will fly to the bow-arm side of the target. Having the wrist too far out will possibly torque the bow so that the arrow flies in the opposite direction, and will certainly put a needless strain on the wrist. So try to apply pressure down the centre-line of the bow. A loose hold on the bow, whether or not a sling is used, will enable the bow to find its own true position.

Aiming

Aiming would seem to present few problems, but there are several points to remember. One is that the angle of the shoulders and arms to the backbone should be maintained at ninety degrees at all distances. This will involve what is called 'unit-aiming'. In this, the position of the upper part of the body is changed at full draw, the change of elevation for distance being achieved by movement at the waist level. If the torso is kept vertical and only the arms moved up and down, alteration in draw-length will ensue. One can see the application of unit aiming in the photograph on page 52 of the archer shooting at the clout in the traditional style. The same principle should be employed at shorter ranges.

Another point is that no one can hold the bow as steadily as if it were locked in a vice. According to archers' individual physical and nervous make-up there will be a certain amount of 'wander', but this is not usually so extreme as to make good shooting impossible. One can still choose the moment to loose when all is correct. Again, if archers always shot their arrows exactly where they were aiming, their scores would rocket immediately, but it is correct shooting that ensures high scores; good aiming with bad technique is useless. Too great a concern with aiming combined with neglect of technique can so affect an archer's shooting that he may become unable to bring himself on to aim before he feels ready to shoot, with the result that he freezes off aim, or snap-shoots as the sight is snatched on to the mark. It is essential that the sight be held on the mark without anxiety by the archer for an appreciable length of time while he concentrates his attention on achieving a perfect loose. To allow the picture of the sight against the mark to trigger off a spasmodic loose is fatal to good shooting. The cure for this is to keep separate the action of aiming from the action of loosing by building in a further stage, such as balancing the weight of the bow across the shoulders and increasing the pressure of the string slightly on the chin. But the habit, once established, is hard to break, so it is as well not to let it develop at all.

Some archers turn to the clicker to enable them to aim and stay on aim until they are given the audible signal to shoot. This works well, but archers often become utterly dependent on the clicker and find they cannot shoot without it. Even so, there is no doubt in my mind that the device has enabled many archers to continue shooting and to enjoy shooting who would otherwise have abandoned it in despair. Remember, then, to avoid this not uncommon complaint, and always to keep aiming separate from loosing.

Relaxation

The difficulties described above are closely connected with tension, both nervous and physical. Nervous tension will become physical, so it is important to keep the mind concentrating on the job in hand to the utmost without letting it become clouded by anxiety. Think about the arrow you are about to shoot, not the previous arrow, whether bad or good. Consider, yes, why the last arrow went where it did, but having made your decision, put it out of your mind and give all your attention to the arrow you are about to nock on the string. How often do moderate archers follow a particularly good end with a miserable failure at the next? Again, we have all seen archers who have hitherto been shooting quite well in a match, put up a bad end or two and go to pieces through anxiety.

Keep the face calm and the neck relaxed or tension will spread over the whole of the body and destroy your control. The more tensed you get, the more effort you will employ and the less steady you will become. Good shooting, though it will not necessarily be easy in fact, will look effortless, just like an expert performance in any other field. Only the performer knows how much concentration is required.

Lastly, to improve you must want to improve. You must be concerned about your shooting when your scores fall below what you expect of yourself. If you just shrug your shoulders and say it was a bad day, you will make no progress. If you shot badly there must have been a reason. You must determine to find out what it was, but without anxiety. Becoming over-anxious can actually cause the very errors you are attempting to eliminate. Set yourself a standard to reach that is within the bounds of possibility and raise it progressively.

Chapter 8

Competitive Archery

In a sense, all archery today is competitive except perhaps bow-hunting, but even here hunters vie with each other, naturally enough. It is perfectly true that one can get a great deal of pleasure from the use of the tackle, as one can in angling by enjoying the skill of casting and being in the open air in agreeable surroundings even when one does not catch a fish. So, too, with archery, there is undoubted pleasure in the exercise itself and the personal competition – or challenge, if you like – of endeavour to reach the score you have set yourself as being within your grasp. There are some who claim that the prospect of winning does not concern them at all and it must be admitted that many of those who enter a tournament must know that they have no chance whatever of winning any prize awarded for excellence in shooting, but if they are honest with themselves they will admit that they would enjoy their shooting more if they could win or be in the position to win. Again, why keep a score at all if you are not competitive-minded? There is always the desire to put in a better score, lowly though it may be, than some acquaintance whom you like to feel you can beat.

Here, though, we are concerned with competitive archery in the accepted sense of the word, where there is a decided intention to win, to beat the other fellows. Taking part is all very well – we want to win.

Competitions take place at all levels: novices' shoot, club championship, handicap event, county and regional championships, trials and national championships, Continental and World Championships, both Target and Field. There may also be team events.

Competition for the Individual

A vital consideration for the individual archer is that of cost. There is the cost of the equipment that the archer uses. The keen competitor will always be seeking improved equipment or, at any rate, equipment that suits his style of shooting better than that which he has already. In these days of rapid technological advance this will involve him in considerable expense.

Next there is the cost of attending meetings. He will need to attend all the important meetings he can, Championships, International Trials and F.I.T.A. Star Meetings. Entry fees represent only part of the expense; there are also travel, accommodation and meals away from home to be considered.

Then there is the cost of time. Some of these meetings will last more than one day, and others will be arranged mid-week. If he cannot get permission to take optional days off, he may have to forfeit salary. Apart from attending meetings, there is the time spent in practice, and I would say that anyone who wants to reach the top would need to practise nearly every day, not necessarily for very long, but regularly. Unless one is prepared to meet the above costs, one cannot expect to reach the top ranks of competitive archery.

Of course, one may be more than willing to make all the above sacrifices and still not have what it takes to win. After the early training stage, a considerable part of an archer's skill depends upon his mental control. Just as genius is said to be an infinite capacity for taking pains, so brilliant shooting is the result of discipline of the mind so that technique is always under control. It is precisely neglect of this factor that causes so many archers to fall away once the pressure is on. Instead of attending to their shooting, they become anxious about how some rival is doing, whether they are being watched by spectators and fellow-archers, whether some detail of their own technique is at fault. All this is destructive of good shooting–the whole attention must be on the arrow you are about to shoot. It will assist in this if a routine is built up which the archer can follow, stage by stage, to the elimination of all outside concerns and anxieties. No one can maintain full concentration for very long, so it is essential to relax at the time when one is not actually shooting Many people will be able to relax naturally by engaging in quiet conversation with others in the intervals of shooting; those who are more tense by nature can nevertheless practise conscious relaxation. Deliberate relaxation of the muscles, particularly those involved with the face, the hands, and with breathing, will aid calmness of mind. The converse is easily demonstrated. If you grit your teeth, tense your legs, grip the bow so that the knuckles stand out white, you will lose steadiness. If you make an angry savage face, you will start to *feel* angry, too. It is important, then, to keep a calm controlled attitude at all times. It may be that there are some sports where violent demonstrations of anger may do little harm, especially if they relieve built-up tension, but archery is not one of these.

The top-class archer keeps his emotions under control and concentrates his full attention on the matter in hand. He obliterates his surroundings. He may even *like* being watched shooting, even under the eye of the television camera, but when shooting, his concentration on the mark and the aspects of his shooting that need attention are so great that nothing else enters his consciousness – like the archer who shot a ten with his last arrow as an express train roared past not so very far away. When asked: 'Didn't you find that train a distraction?' he replied: 'What train?'

It is particularly important not to be swayed by the effect of the last arrow shot. Poor archers, on getting a good end, often go to pieces out of self-congratulation and tension. Equally, their scores may suffer through despair after a bad end. The great archer thinks only of the arrow he is about to shoot – that's the one that matters each time. He *expects* it to go in the middle, he *will*s it into the middle, and it *goes* into the middle.

It goes without saying that the top-class archer will have complete mastery of his tackle. Good equipment will never compensate for poor technique, and most archers use equipment that is capable of achieving much better scores than they can. Even so, meticulous attention to detail is essential. One archer will experiment for hours tuning his bow, finding the best bracing-height, for example. The ideal bracing-height is that which gives the best performance for the individual archer. So much depends on the individual archer's technique that the manufacturers give maximum and minimum bracing heights. Within these limits, the archer can experiment to find what suits his technique best. If a bow is severely over-braced it will lose cast and a greater strain will be placed on the string on loosing. If it is severely under-braced, cast will be increased but only at the expense of loss of stability and risk of damage to the bow. In both cases the bow will very likely become noisier to shoot. But there will be an ideal bracing-height and the top-class archer will keep a frequent check on this.

Another archer will 'clock' a brand-new set of matched arrows to see if he can detect any variations. This is done by shooting the set and marking on a target-faced chart where each numbered arrow goes. Sometimes a definite pattern emerges. This was very important in the days of wooden arrows, but not without its value even today. Obviously one must be a very consistent archer to be able to benefit from this, but it is consistent archers we have in mind.

Plotting where the arrows fall on first, second and third shot without reference to the numbers on the arrows may well tell the archer something about his own deficiencies, whether postural, or connected with mental discipline or speed of loose.

Experimentation may take place in use of arrows of different specification – arrows of much the same spine may have different diameters and wall-thickness, and one specification be decidely preferable to the others. The weight of arrows is important, too.

Another archer will keep several identical sets of arrows, use one for practice, and reserve a set in perfect condition for a tournament. After the tournament, the tournament set go back into practice, while a practice set is entirely overhauled, refletched with the utmost care and set aside for future use in the next tournament.

One need hardly mention the importance of strings, spare strings being kept in perfect condition and 'shot in', so that there is no variation on sights required if a new string needs to be taken into use.

The same care and attention is extended to every part of the archer's tackle. If he has complete confidence in this, he can give his full attention to his technique.

The top-class archer will be dedicated to his sport. He will not only practise assiduously; he will also think, talk and live archery all day long. For him archery will be a way of life, rather than a recreation or a sport. No aspect of archery will be outside his interest, even though he may concentrate on one branch of it. When a conflict of loyalties occurs he will put archery first, but in fact he will endeavour to ensure that no conflict can arise.

Although physical fitness is not so vital in archery as in some other sports, it is nevertheless extremely important. While accurate shooting is the result of skill, physical strength is valuable, too. The stronger one is, the better one can control a bow if one sets about it in the right way. Again, the ability to use a heavy bow competently may be a decided advantage – on windy days, for instance – and at any time a flatter trajectory will mean that the effect of some errors will be reduced. Weight-training and exercises suited to the skill of archery can do nothing but good.

Over and above all this is the will to win. If you have an over-riding desire to win, coupled with a strong sense of fair play and appreciation of the skill of others, and the discipline of mind that enables you to fight to the last arrow of the last end without becoming over-anxious, then you have what it takes to become a top archer.

Team Competition

Archery is not strictly a team game, but a sport in which individual scores may be combined for the sake of team competition. The team is sometimes selected before the shoot, and sometimes the best scorers from a club or county are nominated as the team after shooting has finished. There is much more stress placed upon the individual in the former case, since he knows that if he makes a poor score his team must suffer; the latter case provides an incentive for the modest shot who may be able to oust a member of what would normally be the selected team. There is no necessity therefore to select members who think and act alike, or whose styles match and complement each other. But it is essential that the members of an archery team should be in harmony with each other and full of concern for each other's happiness and well-being. To ensure this is the responsibility of the selectors, the manager and the captain alike. The captain does not have the same powers or responsibilities as the captain in a game like cricket, where the decision to declare or change the bowler may have far-reaching results, but his task is the vital one of maintaining morale on and off the field. A good team is a well-knit community of individuals who respect each other, are good humoured, put the best interests of the team foremost and resolve to behave in such a way as to enhance the reputation of the body they represent.

It is unwise, therefore, to select a team on the basis of the evidence of high scores alone; there are so many other considerations. A better idea is to short-list a number of possibilities, at least twice as many as will be required for a team, and form a squad that will undergo training under experienced coaches. Coaches of this calibre should not have any narrow notions as to how an archer ought to shoot, but should concentrate on ironing-out inconsistencies and acclimatising the squad to top-level competition.

At certain sessions, cine-film can be shot so as to examine every detail of each archer's technique. The use of polaroid cameras will be valuable, too, partly to convince the archer that the observations of the coach are correct, and partly to form a reference file of progress over a longer period. When the squad can be gathered together at the same time, groups can be set to compete against each other in close company, so that the pressures that build up during competitive shooting can be studied and reduced by experience. If you are to beat all-comers, you must first be able to beat those on your own target.

In the squad, competition will always be present, for there is the ever-present knowledge that some will be selected and others left out of the final team, and there is always the chance of a new-comer earning a place on the squad to replace one who is failing to make a satisfactory response.

Furthermore, all members of the squad should be required to return all scores made in competition, including those where there has been some loss of form, with notes on weather conditions, etc. Whenever possible, they should endeavour to attend important meetings where they can be put on the same targets or adjacent targets, if the organisers can conveniently arrange for this.

A good deal can be done, too, by occasional talks by experts on, say, nutrition, anatomy, psychology, physiology, to name only a few useful avenues of approach.

The Team Manager

When selection has been made and a captain appointed, preferably a shooting member of previous experience in the relevant type of event who will be respected by the tean, and essentially one whose temperament is such as to enable him to shoulder responsibility without detriment to his own shooting, the task of the team manager begins. It is helpful if he has been one of the selectors and is well acquainted with the team he will manage.

His first task will be to ensure adequate funds, for the team will have enough to contend with without concern over finances. Next is the question of uniform if this is not already laid down. Not only should it be smart, so as to give the wearers a sense of pride and solidarity, but also suitable for the climate where the event is to take place. Then arrangements must be made for accommodation of a satisfactory standard, and travel by convenient routes and form of transport, keeping in mind the possible adjustments to bookings brought about by the attendance of those who will wish to share rooms. One cannot be dogmatic about the presence of husbands and wives of shooting members. If all goes well, they can be of great assistance and support. On the other hand, such partners could be emotionally disturbing in some circumstances. In the absence of any definite laid-down policy, it would seem best to leave it to the good sense of the team members concerned who best know how they are likely to react.

The Team Manager should be an experienced archer and if he is a coach as well, so much the better. There will be many occasions when his duties will involve knowledge of the rules and of past procedure. The captain and the manager, ideally, can work in close co-operation and each relieve the burdens of the other. As regards the coaching aspect, I do not mean that a coach would be continually advising the archer on how to shoot, far from it–the previous training should have been sufficient, but I do know from experience that a coach can be of great assistance to an archer, just by his presence, or by giving moral assurance and recommending perseverance, positive thinking, and dissuading him from ill-considered adjustments to tackle or style that one is liable to attempt when performance falters.

In the de-briefing after the event, he will also know from his own observations what weight to give to various aspects of conditions and performance.

Travel should be arranged so that the team can have sufficient time to relax and become acclimatised before the event, and opportunities taken for relaxation during the period of the event–swimming, for instance, or sight-seeing. As regards food and drink there are two aspects to consider. One is that the food and drink that is the speciality of the country may not be suitable to the visiting team. Here it is as well not to depart too far from what has been customary at home. The other is that under the stress of competition digestive trouble is very liable to arise. Apart from tournament nerves having an effect, there is the problem that it is not always convenient to get food when it is needed because of the demands of the shooting programme no matter how well this is arranged. Here I would definitely recommend some provision of liquid foods of high nutritional value as a supplement or alternative to other forms of diet. Experience in sports other than archery bears out their great value.

As regards alcohol, unless regulations forbid it, my view is that one is well advised to make no change in one's usual intake. Much the same applies to sleep; if one is not accustomed to going to bed early, I see no advantage in doing so because there is an important shoot on the next day. One may only lie awake fretting, which will do more harm than good.

Apart from his official duties, the manager should be a buffer (but not an old buffer!) who will protect the team from anxieties, who will overcome unexpected difficulties, and free the captain to perform his function as the leader of the team on the field.

Chapter 9

Variety in Archery

The forms of archery are briefly as follows:
Target
Hunting
Field
Flight
Clout
Popinjay
Archery Golf
Archery Games
If an archer wishes to reach the heights of achievement in any one of
these he will obviously do best to concentrate on it to the exclusion of
other forms, if only to allow himself more time to practise, but most
archers will derive greater pleasure from their sport from taking part in
any or all of them, even though only one may be particularly favoured.
There may even be advantages in some ways carried over from one form
to another. For the precise rules for each of these refer to the rule books.

Target Archery

Because it has been well organised as a sport for many years, Target
Archery is the most popular form of archery in Britain. It also has the
advantage that it is not difficult to find a club in most well-populated
areas, and the ground required is not large, though often hard enough
to find and hire. No great experience or trouble is involved in providing
the facilities for shooting. The coaching organisation is well established
in this branch of the sport. Again, some of the other forms are sufficiently similar in technique to enable the archer to take them up after
learning target shooting, but are hardly likely to wean him away from it
entirely because of the reduced opportunity.

Within what may be properly called Target Archery there is considerable variety. Most of this is involved with the different distances shot and the number of arrows shot. There are the traditional British rounds shot at distances measured in yards, and the F.I.T.A. rounds shot at metric distances. With the increased competition in international archery the latter are growing in popularity. Invariably the longest or longer distance is shot first. We are told this is because target archery is a development via Clout of archery used for military practice. Shooting in battle would begin at the longest range and continue if the enemy continued to advance.

So the York Round, for example, consists of 6 dozen arrows at 100 yards, 4 dozen at 80 yards and 2 dozen at 60 yards. The reason for the distribution into 6, 4, and 2 dozen is that when the round was first instituted it was expected that approximately the same total score would be achieved at each distance. Shooting skill has so much improved since then that this no longer holds good. The round is shot on a 4 foot face, divided into 5 zones, scoring 9, 7, 5, 3 and 1.

The F.I.T.A. Round for Men, on the other hand, is equally distributed. It comprises 3 dozen arrows at 90 metres, 3 dozen at 70 metres, 3 dozen at 50 metres and 3 dozen at 30 metres. Here the two longer distances are shot on faces 122 cms. (4 feet) in diameter, and the two shorter distances on faces 80 cms. in diameter, but the faces are divided into ten zones, scoring 10 to 1.

All target rounds recognised by the G.N.A.S. are based on the above principles, but many of the rounds take less time to shoot, where they involve fewer arrows and shorter distances.

Archers' scores are increasing so rapidly that it may not be long before modifications in the rules may be necessary to decide the winners. If maximum possible scores are made by several archers, how do you decide the winner? Already smaller faces are in use for indoor shooting. Not all target archery contests are decided, however, on the total score. In traditional long-bow tournaments the first award goes to the archer with the most hits. And mention must be made of the Antient Scorton Arrow, first shot for in 1673, where the captain and winner of the Silver Arrow is the archer who is the first to pierce the inner gold.

Archery tournaments usually include team events, where the teams are either nominated in advance, or selected from the top-scoring archers eligible.

The individual archer, no matter what his ability, always has the incentive of improving his own handicap rating or classification. Many clubs hold monthly handicap meetings. According to an archer's current standard of ability an adjustment is made to his actual score at the end of the shoot. Under certain conditions a club can apply to the G.N.A.S. for a Handicap Improvement Medal and award it to the archer who has improved most in the season.

Hunting

I have had little experience of this form personally, and the G.N.A.S. is not concerned with its promotion. Opportunity to follow it in Britain is very limited, unlike other countries, such as the United States, where hunters outnumber target archers by far.

Observance of the game laws and the hunter's code of conduct are obviously necessary. Provided one has no moral objections to the use of the bow for killing, bow-hunting must be the most satisfying form of archery there is, using the bow in the way it was originally intended. A high proportion of the skill involved is certainly concerned with the stalk and the recognition of signs, but shooting skill is far from negligible. Only one opportunity may present itself and the archer who can hit the gold infallibly at 40 yards with a sight, or hit the spot of a field target instinctively at an unknown distance may well miss an animal at approximately the same distance in the heat of the moment when emotion plays so much part.

Bow-fishing is another allied pursuit. The equipment is adapted to the purpose by the use of special arrow-heads, fletching and a spool attached to the bow pointing forward. In aiming one must allow for refraction.

Field

Second only in this country to Target Archery in following and opportunity comes Field Archery which was originally started to give hunters the opportunity of practice in the close season. Many target archers also shoot field.

The first requirement is a sizeable tract of country to which archers have the right of access and from which the public can be excluded or limited to certain well-defined paths. Preferably it should be hilly and wooded or covered with scrub, so that the shooting is enjoyably complicated by hazards and deceptive shots. A field course resembles a golf course in one particular, since although it is much rougher, the archers proceed round the course shooting at different distances overcoming difficulties of lie and terrain.

A field course is usually laid out anticlockwise or in a series of zig-zags. It consists of 28 targets, or, if space is limited, of a unit of 14 targets which are shot over twice. The archers are usually sorted into groups each of which begin on a different target, proceeding round the course to finish at approximately the same time.

Just as there are many rounds in target archery, so there is a variety in Field Archery. Some rounds involve shooting at animal faces; some at roundels. The animal faces may have kill and wound areas, scoring different values according to whether each is hit on first, second or third shot, or have rings with scoring values, the highest scoring zone being set within the animal figure. Roundels are usually black and white and have three scoring zones, the extra aiming spot in the middle now scoring more than the inner surrounding it. For the F.I.T.A. Field Round the aiming spot is black, the inner white, and the outer black. For the F.I.T.A. Hunter's Round the target is all black with a white aiming spot, the scoring zones being delineated only by thin white lines invisible at all but the shortest ranges.

The targets vary in size, too, there being a fixed ratio of sizes to a given round and certain regulations regarding the distances at which these may be set. For instance, a target 60 cms. in diameter would be set at 30 to 60 metres, while one of 15 cms. would be set at 5 to 15 metres.

Again, these distances may or may not be marked. The truly instinctive field archer will not be concerned whether the distance is marked or not. The archer using a sight will be greatly benefited by knowing the exact distance. Hence it is often necessary to distinguish between Barebow and Freestyle Classes.

The number of arrows shot at the targets may vary, too. In some rounds up to 2 may be shot, or up to 3, until a score is registered. In others, 4 shots may be taken at each target, or the number may vary according to the size of the target, with 4 shots for the largest and 1 for the smallest. The shots may well be taken all from one post, or as a series of walk-ups or walk-aways, or the shots may be taken from the same distance but from different posts (the fan shot).

Apart from Freestyle and Barebow sections, organisers of shoots often include sections for long-bow, heavy tackle, and crossbow. Classifications according to ability are provided for as in target archery and give

Plate 11. 1st World Field Championship, Valley Forge, U.S.A. August 1969.

an incentive to every archer to improve his ranking.

It will be seen, then, that Field Archery offers greater variety than Target Archery and more opportunities for individual judgement. On the other hand, in Target Archery, where all competitors are together, there is more opportunity to meet others up and down the line in the intervals of shooting and a higher emphasis on steady ice-cold concentration on accurate repetitive shooting at known distances. You have your choice–and you can choose both!

Flight

The purpose of Flight Shooting, as its name suggests, is to shoot an arrow as far as possible. To this end the equipment and technique is continually being modified. It would be true to say that the technical development of the bow owes more to flight shooting than to any other form. The target bow, for instance, has relatively short working limbs like the flight bow, but separated by a long handle section to enable a longer arrow to be drawn and shot with more steadiness. Again, flight shooting offers an admirable testing ground for new bow materials since they are under such severe stress.

Because of the need for a very fast cast, flight bows are short, powerful and severely recurved. A long draw with a short light arrow is made possible by the attachment of a sipur, or kind of shelf, which enables the arrow to be drawn inside the bow. The fletchings are reduced to the minimum, and the sharpness of the loose is increased by the use of a flipper or loosing hook. It is advisable, too, not to hold at full draw which allows the bow to lose power, but to take the arrow back to its full limit and release in one action.

A word here about elevation and its application to both clout and flight shooting.

Flight Angle

For a missile to reach its greatest range an angle of 45 degrees to the horizontal is the optimum in a vacuum, the only factor acting on the missile being that of gravity. But that is in a vacuum. We have also to consider the effects of loss of velocity caused by air-resistance. The greater the initial velocity, the flatter the ideal trajectory will be. A head wind increases air resistance; a following wind reduces it.

Plate 12. George Thorley, Master Flight Shot and Bowyer, using one of his own flight bows.

A bullet of muzzle-velocity 2,000 feet per second has an optimum angle of $37\frac{1}{2}$ degrees to the horizontal. For bait-casting, the ideal angle is 30 degrees, but here we have line-drag to consider. I have no figures for the angle of a golf drive for maximum distance, but from observation I am sure it is much less than 45 degrees.

An arrow does not behave quite the same as a bullet. For one thing its initial velocity is much slower, certainly not more than 250 feet per second from a good bow. For another, its fletching causes drag. From my own experiments, I have proved that there is very little difference in the distance of target arrows shot from 35 degrees to 45 degrees. A good deal depends on the size and type of fletching. If you don't believe it, try it and see for yourself.

However, this is not the end of the story. A target arrow is not the same as a flight arrow. The flight arrow may have a barrelled shape, much smaller flights and a point of balance behind the centre. This means that a levelling-off takes place at the top of the trajectory allowing the arrow to glide on further than it otherwise would. Therefore the ideal angle for flight shooting with flight arrows may well be between 42 degrees and 48 degrees. There is room for much more research into this.

Sheer power of the bow, though important, is not the only factor to consider. There is also the arrow itself, the judgement of angle, the sharpness of loose, and direction, too, for several yards may be lost by an arrow that is not shot straight. A good flight archer can certainly send the same arrow further than the inexperienced one with the same bow and draw-length.

Often events are divided into classes, according to sex, weight of bow, target bow or flight bow, and style of shooting. A 'target' bow is one with which the archer has shot at least two standard rounds. In this class archers must use their own length standard arrows.

In the freestyle class the archer need not hold the bow in the hand. He may use the feet. The distance measurement is taken at right-angles to the range lines at 50 yard intervals, which are themselves parallel to the shooting line, so direction of the shot is important.

The distance of 1,861 yards has been achieved in the freestyle class and 856 yards in the flight-bow (hand-held) class. Archers may classify as Master Flight Shots or First-class Flight Shots.

Clout

Clout Shooting has its origin in the military practice of medieval times. The archers were collectively known as 'the artillery' and were used in battle to destroy the enemy at long range if possible. Though sheer weight of fire-power could do great damage, accuracy was highly regarded, too, so the practice was to shoot at a clout, or piece of clothing or cloth, at 180 yards or more. Old Double in Shakespeare's 'Henry IV, Part II' is said "to have clapp'd i' the clout at 12 score", but maybe Justice Shallow was 'drawing the long-bow' himself, or exaggerating, when he said this.

Such ancient societies in Britain as The Woodmen of Arden and the Royal Company of Archers, the Queen's Bodyguard for Scotland, shoot their own clout rounds. The G.N.A.S. makes provision for men to shoot at 8 to 10 score yards, and ladies from 6 to 8 score.

Shooting may be either one-way or two-way (i.e. with a target at each end of the field). There are five scoring zones on the ground circularly

Plate 13. Les Scott of Maidenhead Archers using the high-kisser technique in clout shooting.

around the clout (now a light-coloured flag) scoring 5, 4, 3, 2 and 1, but the two innermost zones are relatively smaller than might be expected, the radii being 18ins., 3 ft, 6 ft, 9 ft, and 12 ft.

Good judgement of elevation, aim-off in a cross-wind and precise technique can ensure that an archer scores with all his arrows. The fact that an archer has a choice of two elevations except when the clout is set at his maximum range is shown by the following diagram:

Fig. 12. Trajectory.

Where (a) is the maximum distance his bow can shoot, both (b) and (c) can give aim on the clout at (d). With (b) he will be less likely to shoot over or under the distance, but he is much more likely to be affected by wind-drift than with (c). His stance may be more difficult to maintain correctly too.

The fascination of clout shooting is undoubtedly gained from the longer flight of the arrow and the uncertainty of the score until the target is actually inspected. One can often see the arrows falling true for line yet find one has undershot or overshot the target when one goes up to it. Yet how satisfying to see the flag flutter and know for sure that you have hit it at such great range!

Popinjay

Popinjay, which consists of shooting down feathered 'birds' from a tall mast may have had its origins in shooting at actual tethered birds. However that may be, the term is the old English word for parrot and the 'birds' today are brightly fletched with feathers.

In Britain, the Kilwinning Papingo is the oldest traditional contest of

Plate 14. Popinjay Mast.

Plate 14a. Popinjay Technique.

this kind. A wooden figure of a bird with detachable wings is set on a pole projecting from the Abbey tower. The present trophy of the silver arrow was instituted as long ago as 1724, but the records show the Papingo was shot at long before that.

It is not often a Popinjay mast can be set up for it is 90 feet in height, though in Belgium, where this form is popular, some permanent masts are maintained and some popinjay shoots are arranged in lanes horizontally instead of vertically.

The 'birds' are feathered wooden cylinders to be knocked off their perches by an archer shooting up from the foot of the mast. The arrows are fitted with blunts $\frac{3}{4}$ in. to 1 in. in diameter for the sake of safety. Points are scored when a 'bird' is dislodged according to its value–the Cock Bird at the top scoring 5 points against 3 for one of the four Hen Birds, and 1 point for one of the twenty-four or so chicks.

Under any other circumstances shooting straight up is highly dangerous, so there is particular satisfaction in being enabled to do so in controlled conditions.

Archery Golf

This is an attempt to enable archers to compete with golfers over a golf course on more or less equal terms. This is rather more than an archery game, however.

There is a claim, probably apocryphal, that golf stemmed from archery. Certainly golf has an ancient origin and is similar in a way to the archery practice of Rovers where archers used to pick chance marks in open country to shoot at. The most successful archer chose the next shot. Finsbury Fields in London was at one time the most famous centre for Rovers.

Today archers compete with golfers by shooting over the same course. They may use only one bow, but may use any arrows. It is convenient to have a light arrow with small fletching for 'driving', a target or field arrow for 'approach', and one fitted with a spike for 'putting' so as to minimise glances off the green at close range. The archers 'hole out' by hitting a white cardboard disc 4 ins. in diameter. An arrow landing off the fairway or in a bunker incurs an extra stroke, or otherwise the archer would not be at a disadvantage compared with the golfer in a like predicament.

Under these conditions a close-matched game can be played. A very good golfer can out-drive an archer with a target bow, since his ball will usually run on after pitching, often by 100 yards or more. The archer's approach is usually better than the golfer's, but there is not much difference in putting between good archers and good golfers. A field archer has the edge over the target archer in this event since he is more used to shooting at unmarked distances from deceptive 'lies'.

Archery Games

By this, I mean games played on a target face devised to resemble a game such as darts, snooker, snakes and ladders, cricket, noughts and crosses and so on, but few of these allow for competition with the actual players of the game concerned. In darts, however, a match can be arranged, the darts players throwing on to their own board at their normal distance, while the archers shoot at a darts face 2 ft. 6 ins. in diameter from at least 15 yards. The fact that the archer can aim precisely gives him a decided advantage, otherwise.

In addition to the above there are demonstration tricks such as balloon bursting, wand-splitting (worthy of more serious competition, as of old) which are popular at fêtes, but which otherwise do not engage the archer's serious attention.

All in all, it can be seen that variety in archery is extremely wide and can offer a challenge to most tastes.

Chapter 10

Archery for the Handicapped

There is practically no type of physical handicap that will prevent a determined person taking up the sport. In most cases morale will benefit, and in many cases the physical exertion will assist recovery or train the handicapped person to develop new muscles and co-ordination in a way that will enable him to be more adept in spite of his handicap. Nevertheless, since in a few cases it is conceivable that some harm might be done to a handicapped person by well-meaning but ignorant enthusiasts, it is always advisable to check with the medical or surgical staff who know the case-history of the person concerned, before undertaking tuition. In many hospitals and rehabilitation units today archery is on the programme and the G.N.A.S. offers a Certificate of Competence to Physio-therapists who have satisfactorily undergone a course of training.

The Basic Method of Instruction is still a useful system to keep in mind, but one must be prepared to abandon or modify details in order to achieve satisfactory results. For example, the V-draw whereby the bow is brought from the prep. position in front of the archer to the full draw position is very satisfactory for fit archers. But for paraplegics sitting in a wheel-chair without power in the lower limbs a very high degree of balance is required. A better method for them to adopt is to use a prep. position where the bow, as yet undrawn, is placed at head height with both elbows held at right-angles. In this position the archer is balanced comfortably and does not need to alter his balance as the bow is drawn. This is known as the Modified Upper Draw. I should add, however, that the V-draw could be of value for paraplegics if the object of the exercise is to train them to improve their ability to maintain their balance.

I said earlier that archery can improve the morale. The fit person can scarcely imagine the joy and satisfaction to handicapped persons on

Plate 15. Ada Nightingale of Crowthorne Archers.

finding that, when participation in so many sports is denied them or severely limited, archery is one in which they can often compete on equal terms with those who are fit. Even when this is not possible there is a real sense of achievement at being able to shoot moderately well considering the extent of the injury, or even in being able to shoot an arrow at all.

In my opinion handicapped archers are a positive benefit to a club. They are rarely in need of close attention, taking a pride in being independent; their ability to take a share in the organisation of the club as, say, record officers, equipment officers, or treasurers, is unimpaired. This sense of equality is of the very greatest value to the handicapped. One of the things that galls them most is the attitude of ill-informed fit people who seem to think they are somehow different or incompetent. One handicapped archer of my acquaintance tells me that in his employment in a factory he has been obliged to point out to kindly-disposed workmates that it is his legs that are injured, not his mind, when they attempt to explain some simple matter in words of one syllable as if he were incapable of understanding otherwise. In a well-organised club the handicapped archer will feel himself to be a full member on equal terms with the rest.

Now let us look at some of the particular types of handicap and see how they can be coped with.

Paraplegia

Since paraplegics usually have the use of their arms, there is rarely any insuperable problem. Sitting in a wheel-chair gives a stable position and the arms and upper body are usually well developed as a result of so much extra work being put upon them in the course of normal everyday movement. The fit archer, though, should not forget the vital importance of balance. He would find sitting down in a chair a most comfortable way of shooting, but he would have the tension of his thighs and legs to preserve his balance, but the paraplegic has to balance himself without any such aid – no mean achievement in itself. Then the alignment of the chair has to be carefully adjusted, but once set, the handicapped archer is allowed to remain on the line when the other archers retire. Other archers are always willing to bring back the archer's arrows to him and to tell him how they fell on the target. A useful gadget is a small cork-board marked out like a target into which pins may be placed to show where the arrows fell. But in most cases the handicapped archer will be able to spot his own arrows in the target with the aid of binoculars. One slight difficulty that can arise, particularly at short distances, is the bow-string coming in contact with the arm of the chair, but chair-arms are usually removable. If not, the use of a shorter bow with a more acute string-angle would probably give adequate clearance.

Certainly the practice of archery is beneficial in developing the muscles of the arms and torso, exercising breathing and expansion of the chest, and sharpening the mind in promoting co-ordination and concentration.

All in all, those in wheel-chairs are quite likely to be able to practise archery with a high degree of success, but much depends on the location of the spinal injury. If the lesion is high, then the use of the arms may be affected.

Hand Injuries

Where there have been injuries to one or both hands, archery may still be possible. The bow may be strapped into the hand if there is loss of ability to grasp it. The string may be drawn by a hook strapped to the drawing arm or a mechanical clutch brought into use. The loosing hook just mentioned is a useful yet simple device: a rounded hook of metal or plastic is engaged in the string just below the nocking point and drawn back in a vertical position. In order to loose, all the archer has to do is to turn the hook to the horizontal position when the string will be released. Thus the archer who has no fingers or no finger control can shoot quite well so long as he can pronate the hand, a fairly broad movement. The shape, size and angle of the hook will require experimentation to get the best results, but if it is fashioned on a bar of $\frac{1}{8}$ in. $\times$ $\frac{1}{2}$ in aluminium, this will not be difficult. The loading of arrows on to the string may in some cases be impossible. If so, then an assistant would be required.

More Serious Injuries

One would at first think that a person without arms would not be able to shoot, and indeed it is so difficult as to be a triumph of determination and skill. But it has been done, so it is worth mentioning here. The archers had already developed very high manipulative skill with the toes and feet, so great that the loading of the arrow on to the string could be achieved with dexterity. The problem was to draw and aim the bow. This was managed by placing the bow on a support not unlike a ground quiver. While the bow was held steady on the rest with the toes of one foot, the toes of the other foot held the string, drew it back and released it. Of course, aiming and elevation had to be instinctive and the length of draw was limited, but even so the arrows could be shot so as to group on the target at 50 yards.

Deafness

In daily life total deafness can be a severe handicap, though with so much hideous noise about one sometimes wonders what are the benefits of being able to hear! In archery the person who cannot hear is at no particular disadvantage, but he has to be on the 'qui vive' for signals audible to other archers. Those engaged in teaching deaf children, for instance, have to devise visual or tactile signals for shooting control. The actual imparting of instruction to those who cannot hear is relatively easy since so much can be done by demonstration – in fact I sometimes recommend prospective coaches of fit archers an exercise in teaching by demonstration and touch alone when they become too wordy in teaching beginners.

Spastics

Here so much depends on the individual case that one must not be too dogmatic. I have known those with a fair degree of control who have been able to shoot safely unaided, but these are few. Most who are able to shoot at all will need very close personal supervision and assistance at all times. Difficulties in holding the bow may be overcome by strapping the bow into the hand. Difficulties in drawing the bow may be obviated by splinting the bow arm and by using special light-weight bows, 14 lbs at 28 ins. Lack of manipulative power in the string hand may be overcome by the use of the loosing hook. Difficulties less easy to overcome are involved with nocking the arrow on the string, placing the fingers or hook on the strings, not dislodging the arrow from the ledge or nocking point, and drawing and aiming with some confidence. Here an assistant will be necessary and he or she would need some knowledge not only of physio-therapy but also of archery teaching.

The Challenge

It is in overcoming handicaps such as the above that the challenge of archery is most evident and high credit is due to those who accept it with such courage and determination, and to those who are dedicated to the task of helping them.

Chapter 11

Junior Archery

By definition, juniors are those who have not reached the age of 18. Sometimes classes for competition put Juniors into various age-groups. Adult clubs quite often welcome juniors, but in some cases have to impose a lower-age limit or to restrict membership to those who are children of members because of lack of adequate supervision. In my experience, though, young people are very ready to accept the disciplines which the safety of the sport demands, and to take a responsible share of the running of the club. They can often serve very efficiently as record officers, or as officers to maintain club equipment.

In school and youth clubs there is need for at least one adult to take responsibility if only because of the large number of juniors taking part at one time, which imposes its own problems. It is highly desirable that such a person undertakes some training before starting a club. This is provided for under the G.N.A.S., for it has instituted a Certificate of Competence for teachers and youth leaders who have satisfied coaches as to their ability to teach juniors in schools and youth clubs. They must know the Basic Method of Instruction and be able to teach it well, and be conversant with the rules of shooting, suitable tackle for juniors, its repair and maintenance, the variety in archery, and be able to demonstrate correct technique at the short instructional distances. I pressed for the introduction of such a qualification and drew up the list of

in the wider sense, or even to be members of the G.N.A.S., for it is recognised that the nature of their duties often prevents them from sparing the time for personal membership of a club. This is particularly applicable to P.E. specialists, who nowadays, quite rightly, have to interest pupils in a very large number of sports and activities, including the Duke of Edinburgh's Award Scheme, in which archery is a recognised activity.

There are archery clubs in all sorts of schools: primary, secondary, preparatory, public, comprehensive, schools for the handicapped, approved schools and so on, and for older students in Colleges of Education and universities.

The Association for Archery in Schools (and related institutions) which I was instrumental in founding, deals with the particular needs of young archers in this context.

Age is not a particular consideration, for equipment is made today in sizes suitable for all ages. There are some young archers below the age of 12 who shoot quite brilliantly at their distances. I would say, though, that the age of 11 or so is the ideal time to begin archery, because it coincides with a natural interest in 'primitive' outdoor activities, and an ability to concentrate and co-ordinate sufficiently to learn a skill.

The problem in schools is not how to arouse sufficient interest, but how to keep the numbers within manageable proportions. However, once a tradition has been established, the older pupils are particularly vigilant in seeing that the younger ones adhere to the rules and code of behaviour. In my own school where a tradition has grown up in the 30 years I have been running the archery club, I currently have a membership of 60 boys, all with their own personal tackle, and it is hardly ever necessary for me to impose any discipline or rebuke an offender.

At first, though, it is advisable to start a club with some provided tackle to limit the numbers shooting at one time to about a dozen and to be very much in control. It is necessary to impress on the pupils that archery is not a game, but a serious sport, and that the bow is a weapon and could kill or seriously injure if carelessly used.

From the educational point of view, archery is an ideal sport to encourage. For one thing, it can accommodate and encourage those who are unable to participate in other games because of physical disability. Those who cannot time a moving ball (a feature of so many games) often have the qualities of steadiness and determination requisite to become good archers. No pupil is left out of the activity through being denied opportunity by the greater skill of his team-mates as is often the case in team games like football where the poor player hardly touches the ball. It offers admirable exercise in development of the chest and shoulders and encourages deep breathing and muscular co-ordination. Concentration and dedication to the sport is demanded. Even good social habits are inculcated, since one has to participate in setting up the targets and in searching for other people's lost arrows, if only for the sake of continuing one's own shooting. Lastly, it provides a sport that can be carried on into adult life to a greater extent than most. Some special provisions may have to be made. Fortunately a ground is usually available kept in good condition by a groundsman, so the major problem that confronts adult clubs does not exist here. But the school playing fields are in constant use in school time and usually after school and on non-teaching days for matches in other sports than archery, so some definite agreement has to be reached regarding times of use and area provided. The area required for archery should not be less than 50 yards wide by 100 yards long, and there must be some means of preventing access while shooting is in progress, especially if other activities are going on in some other part of the field. One does not want a fielder hotly pursuing a cricket ball in front of the targets. It might be thought that the shorter the distance at which the archers shoot, the less overshot is required, but actually the reverse is the case, since at close range an arrow that flies over the top of the target will be shot at a high elevation. When no other activities are in progress, shooting for distance and at the clout may be permitted under supervision. These branches of archery are particularly popular among juniors. Every boy wants to know how far his bow will shoot: it is better that he should find out under supervision when it is safe to do so, than be tempted to 'have a go' at some other time. Field archery is quite as popular as target archery among juniors and it is simple to make a small course on flat ground, if no rougher country offers, or to set up a few field bosses at various distances as an alternative to the target bosses. Since these butts can be made of compressed cardboard, this can be an economy and provide for more archers to shoot at the same time.

Juniors who take up archery seriously are quite as punctilious in observing rules as adults, but since there may be the occasional irresponsible member of the group, supervision and strict insistence on safety rules are essential. Offences against safety rules should be penalised by expulsion from the club, or at least by a long suspension. One cannot allow fooling about with lethal weapons.

Some schools provide archery on the curriculum, that is to say, as a provided activity in school hours; others allow it to flourish as a club activity under the supervision of a master or mistress out of school hours. Where some tackle is provided it is as well to limit the numbers of participants at any one time to enable the sharing of one set of tackle among not more than three pupils, or those waiting a turn will be liable to cause distraction.

Thus for a group of twelve, four, or better six, bows will be needed. It is much easier to organise a school club where the archers provide their own equipment. This need not be expensive. The equipment suitable for youngsters of twelve or so years of age can be quite reasonable in cost, less in fact than the cost of articles such as cameras, bicycles, fishing tackle, flying model aircraft, which the youngsters might have opted for as an alternative by way of a birthday or other present. Moreover, solid fibreglass bows and alloy practice arrows may be sold to other aspiring members, when outgrown, for a fair price which will offset the original cost. School clubs suffer in one way, in that when an archer has become skilful and able to take responsibility he is liable to leave school; but on the other hand there is the benefit of a steady assured influx of new members year after year.

Suitable tackle for schools is readily available from specialist suppliers and the teacher in charge should insist on getting the recommended articles, either direct or through the Supplies Office. What he should guard against is being persuaded to accept unsuitable tackle from local sports shops who may supply other goods for schools sports departments. They may be well able to supply suitable gear for games such as football, cricket, hockey and tennis, but lack the demand to hold a sufficient stock of fibreglass bows and alloy arrows. If they are willing to undertake the supply of the recommended tackle, though, well and good. One must bear in mind the rapid rate of growth of juniors and get both bows and arrows that are big enough for the bigger pupils. If the weights of the bows are reasonable, the smaller pupils will be able to use them satisfactorily at their shorter draw length.

If the staff in charge are able to devote sufficient time and have the technical know-how, an excellent extension of the shooting practice can be made in the realm of handicraft. It is not difficult to teach handy youngsters to make tackle boxes, target faces, bow-strings, bracers, tabs, ground and hip quivers, and assemble arrows from the components and fletch them. Making wooden or composite bows is possible, too, under the instruction of a craftsman who has the necessary information and interest. Composites, though, involve outlay on fairly expensive materials and a small mistake may mean that the material is wasted and a great deal of time spent in vain, so to avoid disappointment the handicraft teacher is advised to be cautious in undertaking such a project. I have myself found it necessary to do a great deal of the work myself rather than have a bow spoilt through ignorance or carelessness. This can be very time-consuming. But all the other articles can be made by young people without close supervision. The satisfaction of creating a useful and beautiful piece of equipment and of using it effectively is incalculable.

It is easy to see how archery projects can be carried over into other subjects than handicraft, notably mathematics, physics, history and art.

Rightly or wrongly, competitiveness is a feature of our society and of school life. Be sure of this, youngsters will compete with each other, whether you want them to or not. So we might as well make use of this characteristic in the promotion of archery. A school championship can be held once a year, preferably in the summer term after exams have been held. Where there is a House system, House teams can be selected and trained by House archery captains and a competition run as part of the tournament. If other schools not too far away also practise archery, actual matches can be arranged. If not, entry can be made to the postal leagues, both in the regular adult leagues and in the schools postal leagues. The advantage of the latter is not only that the competition is restricted to archers of a similar age-group and ability, but also that the rounds are arranged with the school time limitations in mind. For instance, the A.A.S. Longer Postal Round (for under 18's) is only two dozen arrows at fifty yards and one dozen at forty yards, and the A.A.S. Shorter Postal Round is only two dozen arrows at forty yards and one dozen at thirty yards. This enables archers to shoot in the limited time available in school hours. Again, they are permitted to shoot as often as they like, under organised conditions, in the month for competition and to submit the best score they manage individually to make. This takes into account the difficulty of getting a full team together at any one time in the face of other school activities and of timetable requirements.

Competition of this sort is ideal, for not only is there rivalry with the opponents, but also rivalry to get into the team selected by virtue of score. It means a lot to a youngster to get into a team, whether that team wins or loses.

Monthly handicap shoots can be run with small token awards, such as differently coloured tassels, held for the month by the more successful contestants. A G.N.A.S. affiliated club can, under certain conditions, apply for a Handicap Medal for annual award. There can also be

competition in the making of equipment, the best decorated quiver or the best set of field arrows, and so on – the possibilities are unlimited. Nowadays, most target tournaments and field shoots provide for junior sections, and pupils should be encouraged to enter and be assisted by being afforded transport. One of my greatest pleasures is to take a team to an open event, and to watch both their skill and their impeccable behaviour on the line. Those that have success in such events are often willing to work for and set aside money to get good tournament tackle – and why not? It gives them great pleasure and satisfaction. Rounds for juniors: juniors can, it is true, shoot all the rounds that adults shoot, but some of the younger ones cannot use bows of sufficient power to perform effectively at the longest distances. Accordingly, there is a number of rounds specially devised for juniors in which the distances are graded to suit different age groupings. The best known of these today are the Bristols, based on the distribution of arrows required for the men's York and the ladies' Hereford Rounds as follows:
Boys under 18, Bristol I @ 80, 60, 50 yards
Girls under 18, Boys under 16, Bristol II @ 60, 50, 40 yds.
Girls under 16, Boys under 14, Bristol III @ 50, 40, 30 yds.
Girls under 13, Boys under 12, Bristol IV @ 40, 30 20 yds.
There is the same kind of provision for Metric rounds based on the F.I.T.A. Rounds. Also there are older rounds, such as American, Western, Windsor, Short Windsor and St. Nicholas, which are quite suitable for juniors.
In field archery the lesser power of juniors' bows is allowed for, and shorter distances are permitted at some targets, by means of forward posts, though the juniors proceed round the same course as the adults and in company with them. Juniors under 18 and over 15 shoot precisely the same courses as the adults under G.N.A.S. rules and are quite able to do so.
Competition is possible at all levels. Counties, Regions and the national body all organise their own junior championships. Junior International matches have been organised in Britain (twice) and in Denmark and more will follow. Every year, too, junior scores are submitted for the Junior Mail Match organised by F.I.T.A., each member nation deciding on the month from which its juniors will submit their scores.
In the school club, the older and more experienced archers should be encouraged to take positions of responsibility as captain, vice-captain, records officer, secretary, equipment officer and so on. Before they leave

school, it is advisable to get them to join a local adult club, as well as the school club, so that continuity is ensured when they leave school Most clubs will readily accept young people who have been well trained in archery, and may well benefit from attracting their parents, too. My own adult club has for many years had an intake of senior pupils, parents, old boys and their girl friends and their wives. All parties benefit.

Archery in schools and youth clubs is growing, aided by teachers who are enthusiasts, by coaches who train teachers for the Certificate of Competence and by students from Colleges of Education and Universities, who, having been introduced to it and received training carry it on in the schools where they go to teach. The fees for affiliation of a school or youth club composed entirely of juniors except for officials in charge are extremely low, and is not increased no matter how large the club is. The effect of this encouragement is already being found in the field of international competition. The best of our juniors are challenging and beating their elders at all levels in archery as in other sports. Good luck to them!

Chapter 12

Care, Making and Maintenance

The more care that is taken in the use and storage of equipment, the less maintenance and repair that will have to be done. This applies no less to club equipment than to personal tackle. There should be a club officer appointed to see that club equipment is kept in good order, but it is every club member's responsibility to see that it is not misused or left lying about. After all, he pays for it–in part.

Bows

The less bows are knocked about the better. This particularly applies to composites, where a serious flaking of the fibreglass can result from a chip or a knock, but all bows should be treated with care, since they are highly stressed in use. They are best kept in a bow-case when not in use and on the ground quiver or bow-stand while shooting is in progress. If they get wet, they should be dried off before being put away. An occasional wax-polishing will help to preserve the finish.

Bracing and unbracing should be done by the conventional push-and-pull method shown on page 32. The step-in method is not so good since it may cause twisting of the limbs if carelessly performed, but done properly with the pressure of the buttocks on the handle and with the supporting instep raised to prevent twisting of the limbs, it is all right. If one has difficulty in bracing a bow by the conventional method, one can always ask for assistance or use a 'bow-stringer'.

Solid fibre-glass bows do not need much attention except to see that the ledge has not been worn away and that the handle has not moved from its place. If the ledge is worn, a rest may be attached to the bow. Indeed it is a good idea to attach one anyway, as it reduces friction. Keep a bow supported on pegs or hung up in a cool dry place. It is inadvisable to stand it on end.

I will not go into the manufacture of composite or other bows although I have made many and know many archers who have made successful bows, since it is a skilled job and warrants a more detailed study than is appropriate here.

Lastly, try to avoid having a string break on the bow or using a string that is of the wrong length.

Strings

Signs of a string being likely to fail are the fraying of the strands, the actual parting of a strand, or loss of bracing-height. On seeing such signs you should replace the string.

Dacron strings made to the same specification do not always behave the same at first owing to the slightly greater elasticity of the newer string, so 'shoot in' your spare strings or you may spend some time finding a new sight-mark. Always have at least two strings to your bow with nocking points marked and built up as necessary.

Properly made Kevlar strings with negligible elasticity should shoot exactly the same as the old ones.

A little light waxing of Dacron strings is advisable not to keep damp out, because they are impervious to moisture, but to keep the strands conveniently together.

The loop-serving and the centre-serving of 'endless' strings may fray or slip. This in turn can cause the nocking-point to shift. If so, it is necessary to serve them again. An application of an impact adhesive under the serving may prevent slipping, but one should consider the effect of the glue on the string fibre. I have not found the impact adhesives I have used to be in any way harmful, but I cannot answer for all. It must be an impact adhesive that never dries brittle, but remains flexible. Any glue that dries hard would, of course, be worse than useless, since it could sever the string fibres.

Soft-twist or braided nylon is ideal for Kevlar strings and can equally well be used for Dacron strings. On no account use monofilament on Kevlar strings, but you may if you like use it for the centre-serving of Dacron strings, for it gives a very fast loose. Get the right gauge monofilament to match the number of strands you use in your string and the size of your nocks. Be very exact and firm in serving monofilament, for if it comes loose, the whole serving will unravel in a flash.

Nocking points should be maintained at the right place and thickness, with dental floss on Kevlar strings, or with dental floss or nock-locks on Dacron strings.

If you choose to make your own strings, as many archers do, it is not difficult, but takes time and attention to detail. The number of strands can be decided by reference to the manufacturers' tables, but 12 strands of Dacron B50 would suit most men's bows, or 18 strands of Kevlar (but these figures are liable to change as new and improved materials come on the market).

It is unwise to have a very thin string as it is more likely to break, and will in any case cause unsteady shooting being more elastic, and inclined to 'bounce' on loose. You might also have problems in building up nocking-points and suffering from sore fingers. An extra heavy string will behave all right, but you will lose distance with it, apart from possibly having nocking problems.

For the endless string, make a jig to the following design capable of being extended to accommodate the lengths of string you are at all likely to require.

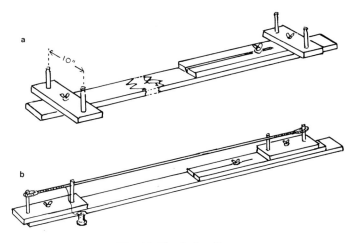

Fig. 13. The String Jig.

Taking an existing string of the required length and same material, turn the pillars into line, put the loops over the outermost pillars and adjust the length of the jig to pull it tight, but not too tight, as a new string may stretch a very little at first. To some extent though, this will be compensated by the firmness of the whipping and the few turns you may put into the string when it is completed. Mark the position of the jig extension, so that you have a permanent record when you come to make other strings for the same bow.

Return the pillars to the position shown in the diagram and wind round the requisite number of strands, half the number down one side, and half the number up the other side. Then when the pillars are brought into line again, there will be the right number together down the string. There must be an even number of strands in the string, of course. Tie off with one reef knot and have this nearly midway between two of the pillars at one end, so that it will be covered by the whipping. Ensure that the strands are all under equal tension and serve on a whipping of nylon thread midway between the pillars at each end and long enough to form the whole of the loops. Finish off by drawing the free end of the thread back under the last half-a-dozen turns. There are several ways of doing this. The easiest to describe is probably this: bind the last few turns over a loop of spare thread, so that the free end can be put in the loop and drawn under.

Turn the pillars back into line again, and adjust the served portions around the outermost pillars. Whip them together in the same way so as to form loops of the required size for the bow as shown in fig. 13b. Remove the string from the jig and try it on the bow. If it is not right and cannot be adjusted by a modest amount of twisting, then you have not estimated the distance correctly and you will have to discard it. But since you have marked the jig, any further strings should be made of the correct length. If you have had no existing string to measure by, the only reliable method of finding out what length you require is to attach an over-long string (such as a single-ended one for a long wooden bow) by means of a timber-hitch. By adjusting the hitch, the correct length can be ascertained.

If the string is of the correct bracing-height according to the bow-manufacturer's specification, or shows half-an-inch of string-groove in the bow when braced, proceed to serve the centre-serving while the bow is braced. Ensure that the string is covered from a point two inches above the nocking point to an extent far enough below it to avoid chafing of the string on the bracer on those occasions (rare, we hope,) when it comes into contact with it. A serving tool makes this job easier, but the thread can be served direct from the reel provided that it is evenly laid with no gaps or overlaps.

Note: Kevlar strings need to be made at least $\frac{3}{4}$ ins. longer than Dacron, for they do not stretch when braced on the bow or when loosed.

Arrows

As may be expected, arrows need more frequent attention than other parts of the archer's tackle.

One essential is straightness. If an arrow is bent, it cannot fly true. Either it will veer off course if the bend is bad enough, or it will wobble in flight owing to uneven rotation and fall short at longer ranges. Then there is the all-important matter of the Paradox. If an arrow is bent, the amount of flexing will be reduced or exaggerated or set into a different direction, and so the arrow will adopt a different flight path immediately on leaving the bow. Spinning on the finger nails or sighting along the shaft while it is rotated often shows up moderately severe bends, but a straightness tester with a micrometer attachment will show that a shaft that appears straight to the naked eye may be quite 5 to 10 thou. out of true.

Experienced archers with good control of strength can straighten arrows moderately well by hand, but it is easy to snap a shaft through carelessness or to make matters worse by putting fresh bends in. 'Little and often' is the best advice I can give in straightening arrows. A straightening aid in the form of a pair of pliers can be used with more confidence, since it is fitted with an adjustable stop that can prevent excessive bending. It is often useful in dealing with bends near the pile end of the shaft, where manual pressure is difficult to apply.

If you decide to refletch a set of arrows completely, you should also check for straightness after cleaning off the old fletching as you can then more accurately see where any bends may occur, particularly at the critical fletching end of the shafts. Even rolling on a really flat surface, such as a marble slab, can show where some bends are present. When it comes to straightness of shafts, near enough is not good enough –perfection is essential. One can make enough mistakes in one's shooting without having to cope with bent arrows as well.

Even so, the straightest arrow can be sent off course by defective fletching. As soon as a fletching becomes 'tatty', dislodged or damaged it should be replaced. With feather fletchings, not only colour should be matched, but also texture, shape and 'wing'. To make a good job it will be better to replace all the fletchings on a shaft rather than to use a poor match to replace one of them.

A rough job in an emergency can be done with cotton carefully wound through the barbs of the vanes so as to hold them in position while the glue is drying, but a fletching jig need not be expensive and much greater accuracy can be achieved. Take care to adjust the jig to match the existing offset if there is any, and to thoroughly clean and 'key' the surface of the shaft. A thin smearing of vaseline on the fletching clamp will help to prevent accidental gluing of the fletching to the clamp. Use a waterproof glue very sparingly and leave the fletching long enough in the clamp for the glue to dry thoroughly.

Fletching angles. For three-fletch the fletchings must be at 120° to each other, with the cock feather at 90° to the nock. For four-fletch it is

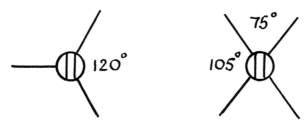

Fig. 14. Fletching Angles.

best to have angles of 75° and 105° so that there is less chance of the fletchings touching the bow than if they were spaced at 90° to each other. Jigs are designed so that these angles can be correctly located.

For really accurate shaping of the feathers on the shaft a feather burner is invaluable.

You will need a transformer, a switch, a jig to hold the arrow nock and shaft, and a piece of resistance wire or metal strip that will get hot when the current is switched on. The wire can be shaped to the feather profile required and over-sized square sections of fletchings already stuck to the shaft can be rotated against it to form perfectly matched fletchings both in shape and in position on the shaft. If the wire is of the wrong resistance and gets bright red hot when the current is switched on you will be in danger of setting fire to the fletchings, but a dully glowing wire will be all right if you rotate the shaft at not too slow a pace. With care, however, ready-cut fletching can be put on accurately.

Plastic fletching of various types, rigid, flexible or slotted, are even

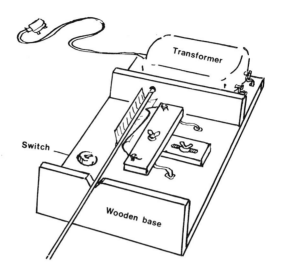

Fig. 15. Feather Burner.

easier to attach, but you must have the right glue to match the plastic of which each is made.

Blunted piles should be sharpened carefully with a file or replaced if badly worn. They can often be removed from alloy shafts by gently heating the tube near the pile. If gentle heat is not effective, leave well alone and let an expert do the job, for too much heat will destroy the shaft.

Nocks are easily replaced, but ensure that they are correctly aligned both in relation to the fletchings and true to the line of the shaft. Make sure, too, that the size of the slot is identical with those in the rest of the set.

Polish and keep clean, avoiding such harsh abrasives as steel wool. To assemble your own shafts is often a considerable economy. The procedure is the same as detailed above. For securing piles, hot-melt resin is good, for it gives good adhesion yet enables the piles to be removed with gentle heat. Shafts are usually available ready nocked and

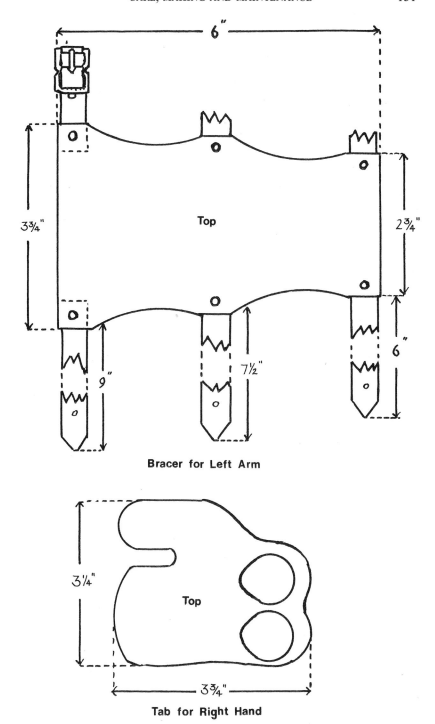

6"

3¾"

2¾"

Top

9"

7½"

6"

Bracer for Left Arm

3¼"

Top

3¾"

Tab for Right Hand

Fig. 16.

piled, the only remaining tasks being fletching, cresting, naming and numbering. The fletching, however, is by far the most important part of the whole assembly.

For one's own pride in workmanship it is worth while making a neat job of the cresting, to use paint that will not easily chip, and to endeavour to get the rings even. This can be done by rotating the shaft in a V-shaped support while the hand and brush are held steady on a bridge. It is useful to arrange that the cresting also serves as a bracing-height gauge, as you will then have a ready check while shooting.

The Rules state that arrows must bear the name or initials of the archer. Apart from identification in the target it is as well to have arrows named, since you are more likely to get a lost one returned.

As regards numbering, as has been stated before, you may the more readily detect a shaft that is not flying true. For Field Archery you must have them ring-marked for number with bands 5 mm wide.

Bracer & Tab

The bracer is best made of fairly stout leather of the kind that is used for brief cases and the like. Thinner flexible leather is needed for the half-inch wide straps attached to buckles and riveted to the bracer by bifurcated rivets $\frac{1}{2}''$ long. To buckle this on to the left arm it is convenient to have the buckles in the position shown.

The tab is made of pony butt or Corfam. The sizes of these two articles are suitable for the average man, and would have to be modified to suit the size of the archer's arm and hand, particularly the tab. Those shown are for right-handers; left-handers would need to make them in the reverse design.

The Quiver

Make this of leather stiff enough to hold its shape reasonably well. It is best to cut a paper pattern and fold it lengthwise along the dotted line to ensure absolute symmetry. Having cut out the parts, thong the edges of the quiver together, inserting the lugs at the points shown, and leaving the broader end open to receive the arrows. The straps, the shorter at the top, are doubled over a belt of convenient size and attached to the lugs by bifurcated rivets. Their length can be adjusted to suit the archer before they are finally fixed. They can be joined to themselves between the quiver and the belt, but leave them free to slide along the belt. If you have enough material, the lugs can be cut out as part of the body of the quiver. It is not difficult to devise an arrow separator to insert in the open end of the quiver, which will hold six arrows comfortably of lengths between 24 ins. and 28 ins.

Target Bosses

These should never be rolled along the ground as rolling loosens the coils of straw rope of which they are made or breaks the edges of stramit. Nor should they be hollowed by the backs of archers carrying them, dropped on edge, or shot at from the wrong side. The best means of transportation is a trolley. A very simple and effective design is a low platform three foot square with brackets to hold four wheel-barrow wheels underneath. Attach a towing bar and you have a means of moving several targets and stands over the ground without difficulty. A steering swivel on the front two wheels is useful, but not essential, as it is quite easy to pull round to the direction required. If targets are carried

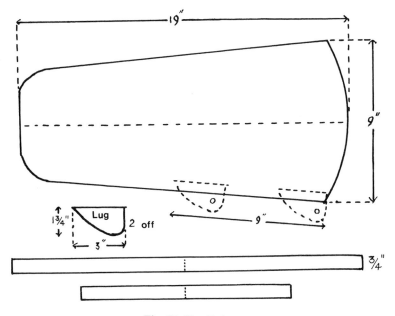

Fig. 17. The Quiver.

on the back they should be held nearly vertical with the hands supporting underneath, not at the sides. In this way the shoulders will not hollow the centres and cause the bosses to 'saucer'.

In use they must always be securely fixed even in apparently calm weather. An unexpected gust of wind can hurl the target to the ground with catastrophic results to any arrows in it. Many pounds worth of damage can be done in this way for the want of a moment's forethought. Probably the best way is to prepare a length of strong cord about 22 feet long. Attach a tent peg in the middle and skewers at each end. Then the skewers can be thrust into the edges of the boss at 10 o'clock and 2 o'clock and the peg driven into the ground behind the target to hold both the stand and the boss firmly to the ground. In rough conditions it may be advisable to tie the target to the legs of the stand and to stake the legs to the ground.

The storage of targets is another concern. Store in a cool dry place, preferably flat. Allow air to circulate between the targets if they have to be put away damp and inspect regularly for signs of mildew that will indicate rotting of the string which holds the rope together and for signs of mice. Mice can do fearful damage to targets, not only by making nests in them, but also by gnawing away at the string.

Eventually, however, the best targets will deteriorate, and there is little that can be done to restore them. A few months' extra life may be obtained by stitching weak places with an upholstery needle, but once the centre coils are shot out, they cannot be replaced. Still, a great deal of the target material can be used where the straw rope is still fairly sound. It may be re-rolled and stitched together like a raffia mat to make serviceable field bosses up to 2 feet in diameter or boxed in wooden frames 26 ins. square. For this, cut the rope into 26 in. lengths, straighten out and whip the ends and cramp them parallel to each other in a box frame of timber 1 in. thick with the aid of carpenter's cramps. A layer of rubberised glue between each strip will make the job more secure. Fix the fourth edge to the frame and reinforce the corners and you will have an excellent butt for field archery. A carrying handle and a strut on the back will enable you to transport it easily and erect it where required.

A very serviceable butt for a permanent field course can be made as follows.

Cut fibre building board into strips 5 ins. wide. Bond or bolt this together, forming a target butt 2 ft. 6 ins. × 3 ft. × 5 ins. To enable arrows

Fig. 18. Boxed Butt.

to be extracted easily, soak the face of the target in thin oil. This will dry in, and will not remain oily to the touch. For best results, weatherproof the whole target by soaking it in creosote before the oil treatment or keep it covered with polythene.

Heavy-duty corrugated cardboard can be lashed together in about 16 thicknesses to form a butt that costs nothing, but it is not easy to extract arrows from such a butt which may also cause bouncers from light bows.

Faces

Faces need to be tautly stretched on the bosses and secured by safe nails or staples that neither project through the boss nor are liable to cause damage to arrows. Care must be taken not to rip the face when handling the target. Once the face has been badly shot up, little can be done to restore it, though a replacement centre can be stuck on suitable only for practice.

Field faces are usually printed on paper which may be 'toughenised' and rendered relatively damp-proof. It is a good idea to paste these onto thin card before use. Not only do they last longer, but they lie flatter and it is much easier to judge the score of arrows that are near the lines.

Stands

These should be substantially made of soft wood to the accompanying design and faced with rubber to minimise damage both to arrows and to

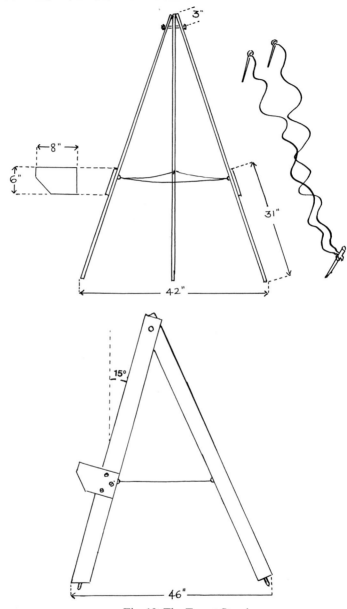

Fig. 19. The Target Stand.

the stands themselves. The supports should be checked to see that they are still at right-angles to the uprights. If they start to give, the target can slide to the ground. The top of the stand also needs inspecting to make sure that the wood by the bolt-holes has not split or been shot away by arrows that have penetrated the target.

Target stand materials:

3 pieces of soft wood 6 ft. × 3 ins. × 1 in.

2 pieces thick waterproof ply-board 6 ins. × 8 ins., screwed and glued.

One 6 ins. × $\frac{3}{8}$ in. coach bolt with washers (in $\frac{3}{8}$ in. hole in centre member, in $\frac{5}{8}$ in. holes in outer members).

Tethering rope: 22 feet of strong cord, 2 metal skewers and 1 stout metal tent-peg.

Rubber for facing front edges of legs.

String or cord for regularising the splay of the legs.

This will make a stand to support a 4 foot target with its centre at 130 cms from the ground. Sawn-off nails driven into the bottoms of the legs will make spikes to push into the ground for greater security.

Chapter 13

The Organisation of Archery

While I could refer the reader to the constitutions and rule books of the bodies concerned and do in fact do so, I know full well that most archers never study them except in part until some dispute arises relating perhaps to finance or regulations, whereupon they claim:

(a)   that a statement supports their contentions and can be waved like a banner to fight under;

(b)   that what it says can be read in such a way as to support their views;

(c)   that it is ambiguous and can therefore be ignored;

(d)   that it says the opposite of what they think it ought to and therefore should be challenged.

Archery is no different from any other sport in this, but a great deal of dispute and bickering could be avoided if more archers accepted their responsibility, studied its regulations and constitutions, and saw to it that these were couched in unequivocal terms when drafted or amended. Annual General Meetings can be boring—there always seems to be too much time spent on reports and not enough on what seems to matter most to the attenders, Any Other Business—but it is here that the ordinary archer should make impact. It is no use grumbling about 'the Establishment' later—he has set up the Establishment either by supporting it or by relinquishing his rights by non-attendance.

Unfortunately reform takes time, especially when a series of committees have to consider a proposition before passing it on with their support, yet this is a needed check to frivolous or ill-considered proposals.

Without going into all the details and alternatives, let me sketch the general pattern of archery at different levels, individual, club, county, regional, national and international.

Individual

Most archery bodies allow for individual, or Ordinary, membership, and though such membership provides some slight privileges, most individual members are club members as well and join in this way to show support of a senior body. A club member enjoys voting powers at Annual General Meetings of his club.

Club

There are today over 860 clubs in Great Britain, either Open, for anyone to join; Closed, restricted in membership; or Junior, composed of those under 18. There are special provisions for Universities, the Disabled, etc. If the club is affiliated, as is usual, to the County, Regional and National organisations, fees to all of these are passed on by the County Secretary/Treasurer to the Regional and National Treasurers.

The constitutions of clubs vary a good deal, but are tailored to suit particular needs. What is certain is that every club is kept alive by the devoted efforts of a small number of enthusiasts who keep things moving and do most of the work.

A club will need a Chairman, Secretary, Treasurer, Captain, Records Officer, Equipment Officer, and possibly other officers. In a small club some of these duties can be covered by the same person. In addition a club should get one or more of its members trained as an Instructor or higher grade of coach.

Usually a club has the right to appoint one of its members as representative to the County Committee. Fees vary a good deal, but are not usually very high. The chief outlay is usually affiliation fees, ground rent and/or maintenance, and provision of beginners' equipment and targets.

In some cases there is no local club to which an individual can belong, but, provided that a sufficient number of like-minded people and a suitable piece of ground can be found, there is no reason why one cannot be founded.

The choice of ground is all-important. For target archery it should be an open area of flat mown grass, ideally at least 130 yards long and 50 yards wide, and sited in such a way that shooting will not be into the sun at likely times of day. Works clubs may be in a stronger position than open clubs in that a recreation ground may be provided, but on the other hand they will have the problem of sharing its use with many other sports clubs attached to the firm, a consideration which will limit the occasions on which it can be used. Open clubs may be able to get information from local Sports Councils. School grounds may be applied for out of school hours, and rugby club grounds may be available during the summer archery season when rugby is not played. For field archery a much larger area of rough ground is required, preferably wooded and hilly, or at least undulating.

It is vital that the public can be excluded from both kinds of club ground, so as to avoid danger to passers-by and interference with the shooting arrangements. Toilet facilities and storage space for targets should either be provided or permission granted for their installation. On the rest of the organisation of a new club, the best advice can be obtained from the County Organiser.

County

Nearly all counties have a county association with a committee largely made up of representatives from the clubs, but with at least a Chairman, Secretary, Treasurer, Coaching Organiser, and very likely other officers, such as, for example, Records Officer, Match Secretary, Newsletter Editor, Field Archery representative. As well as organising archery within its borders, the committee has the right in most Regions to appoint two representatives to the Regional Executive Committee. The fees payable to the County Organisation are usually very small considering the work done directly for the archers.

Region

In the Grand National Archery Society there are nine Regional Societies: The Southern Counties Archery Society, The Northern Counties Archery Society, The Grand Western Archery Society, The West Midlands Archery Society, The East Midlands Archery Society, The South Wales Archery Society, The North Wales Archery Society, The Scottish Archery Association and The Ulster Archery Association. Like the other bodies already mentioned, the Regional Organisation has its committee composed largely of representatives and with other officials as required. It appoints representatives to the National Council of the G.N.A.S. in numbers roughly proportionate to the number of clubs in its Region. Thus, at the time of writing, S.C.A.S. and N.C.A.S. appoint 3 reps. each, and U.A.A. and N.W.A.S. appoint 1 each.

National

The governing body for archery in Great Britain is the Grand National Archery Society, founded in 1861 and its decisions are made either at the A.G.M. or by National Council, composed of the reps. from the Regions, a President, four Vice-Presidents, a salaried Secretary Treasurer, Chairmen of Committees where these are not already Councillors, a Handicap Advisory Officer and a Newsletter Editor. There are twelve Standing Committees, as follows:
Finance, Constitution, International, Coaching, Judges, Target, Field, Target Selection, Field Selection, Flight and Clout, Junior, National Archery Centre. Each of the above deals with the branch of activity that its name indicates, but decisions are made by National Council as a whole, after hearing recommendations.

International

The international governing body for archery is the Fédération Internationale de Tir à l'Arc (F.I.T.A.), founded in 1931. At the time of writing it has 58 member Associations. There is an Administrative Council, an Executive Committee, and six Standing Committees: Rules and Regulations, Field Archery, International Judges, Medical Commission, International Diary and Finance Commission.
The senior administrative body of F.I.T.A. is Congress, held at the time of every World Target Championship and Olympic Games where these include archery. It comprises not more than three representatives from each member association, together with members of the Administrative Council. Each member association has one vote which may be cast by proxy. Each member association pays an annual subscription.

*   *   *

I have purposely omitted many details of the work of each of the above bodies, such as the Championships each organises, in order to make clearer the chain of representation, whereby a member of a club can eventually have a proposal taken to the highest level if it gains sufficient support. It will, however, take a long time unless advantage is taken of short cuts where these are set up to deal with emergencies. The other feature I would like to stress is that although you may naturally have a close loyalty to the smaller organisation whose members you know personally, you will be part of the larger organisations also with a degree of responsibility towards them.

The National Coaching Organisation

There are Instructors and three grades of Coach.

Instructors

Those who have passed the examination as Instructors are issued with certificates valid for three years, at the end of which time they may be renewed. Instructors are chiefly concerned with teaching beginners in their own clubs.

County Coaches

After an Instructor has served for two years, he may apply to take the County Coaches' Examination. If successful, he can obtain a certificate valid for three years. His duties will be concerned with coaching at any level, chiefly in and near his own county, under the direction of the County Coaching Organiser.

Regional Coaches

A County Coach who has served for three years can apply to take the Regional Coaches' Examination. If successful, he will be issued with a certificate valid for five years. He does not necessarily undertake more advanced coaching, but is responsible for training candidates at Instructor and County Coach level, and examining at Instructor level, mostly in his own Region.

National Coaches

These, the highest grade of coach, are appointed by assessment by a panel of National Coaches after satisfactory service as Regional Coaches for at least three years, and have certificates valid for five years. They are, in addition, examiners of all levels of Coach and are empowered to operate anywhere in the country.

It will be seen, then, that National, Regional and County Coaches may all undertake advanced coaching, but the two former grades have specific other duties. Nationals and Regionals will frequently have more experience than County Coaches, but not necessarily, for a County Coach may choose not to proceed any further. All coaching is voluntary – the coach is entirely free to choose how much work he undertakes to do.

The Administrative Organisation of coaching is parallel to this. Most counties have a Coaching Organiser (who may be of any grade). Each Region has a Regional Coaching Organiser (who also may be of any grade). With him as Chairman the County Organisers form a Regional Coaching Committee.

Likewise, the National Coaching Committee is formed of Regional Coaching Organisers with the National Coaching Organiser as Chairman. In addition there is the national Coaches' Registrar. The duties of the Organisers are to organise archery coaching in their respective areas. They usually have a seat on the executive archery committees.

Coaching groups are formed on a county or two-county basis. Meetings provide an opportunity to exchange views and to formulate proposals. From time to time Coaches' Assemblies are held. Any coach or instructor can attend. Such conferences also provide an opportunity for exchange of views and a means whereby new coaching techniques can be demonstrated and discussed. Recommendations can be passed direct to the National Coaching Committee for consideration. This can save a considerable amount of time.

How does this affect the ordinary archer? A County Coaching Organiser will, if possible, arrange for a team of coaches to visit a new club to get it started on the right lines. Members of established clubs can attend coaching courses either residential or non-residential to improve their shooting. They can, if they wish, enrol on an instructor-training course, or get a fellow-member to undergo training. In this way coaching is within reach of all.

So far coaching has the most comprehensive organisation of any department of archery due to the late Bill Dixon's vision and hard work in establishing it. Other developments have followed. The setting up of Regional Judges' Panels and the grading of Judges as being qualified to judge certain standards of event, for instance, but it all depends on the willingness of archers to undertake work on behalf of others. They don't want a great deal of thanks, but they do need to be assured that their efforts are appreciated.

SELECTED READING

Classics

Roger Ascham	Toxophilus
Eugen Herrigel	Zen the Art of Archery
Adrian Hodgkin	The Archer's Craft
Maurice & Will Thompson	How to Train in Archery

History of Archery

Robert Hardy	The Longbow
E. G. Heath	The Grey Goose Wing
Sir Ralph Payne-Galwey	The Cross-bow
D. Roberts	The English Bowmen

Those who are interested in this aspect of the sport could not do better than join the Society of Archer-Antiquaries whose Journal gives results of recent researches.

Tackle-making

'Goldmaster'	Making Bowstrings
Max Hamilton	Plastifacts
Doug Kittredge	How to Make Arrows
Doug Kittredge & Tom Jennings	How to Make Bows

General

E. G. Heath	Better Archery
Mike Smith	Archery
	Know the Game–Archery
National Archery Association of America	N.A.A. Instructors' Manual

Magazines

British Archer } Toxophilus }	bi-monthly British publication
Archery World } Bow & Arrow }	bi-monthly American publication
Archery	monthly American Field publication

GLOSSARY OF TERMS

ANCHOR POINT   Fixed point on archer's face to which string and loosing hand is drawn.

ARCHER'S PARADOX   Peculiarity of arrow flight on passing the bow.

ARCHERY DARTS   Shot on a darts face 30 ins. in diameter.

ARCHERY GOLF   Shot round a golf course against golfers. See G.N.A.S. Rules.

ARROW PASS   Part of the bow against which the arrow lies.

ARROW REST   A shelf above the bow handle on which the arrow rests during the draw.

BACK (of bow)   Part of the bow limb on the opposite side to the string.

BAREBOW   Art of shooting without sights.

BASIC TECHNIQUE   Systematic method of teaching the elements of shooting.

BELLY (of bow)   Part of the bow limb nearest the string.

BEST GOLD   Arrow judged in a contest to be nearest the pinhole.

BLUNT   Arrow with a blunt 'point' for stunning small game.

BOLT   A cross-bow arrow.

BOW ARM   The arm that holds the bow.

BOW-CASE   A sheath for keeping a bow when not in use.

BOW SIGHT   An adjustable device used for aiming.

BOW STRINGER   A device for facilitating the bracing of the bow.

BOW WINDOW   A space between the bow and the string through which the archer may be sighting.

BOSS   Target usually made of compressed straw.

BOUNCER   An arrow that hits the target and rebounds.

BOWYER   One who makes bows.

BRACE   To fix the string into the nocks preparatory to shooting.

BRACER   The equipment worn on the bow arm to keep loose clothing out of the way.

BRACING-HEIGHT   Distance between the string and a specified point on the bow when braced.

BROADHEAD   A killing, bladed arrow-head.

BUTT   A permanent erection of turf, straw bales, or similar material.

CAST   A term used to describe the power of a bow to deliver an arrow.

CENTRE-SHOT   A bow designed to allow the arrow to lie down the centre-line of the limbs.

CLASSIFICATION   The graded measure of an archer's ability.

CLICKER   An audible draw-check, often used as a signal to loose.

CLOCKING   Shooting individual arrows repeatedly, noting where they strike.

CLOUT SHOOTING   Long-distance shooting derived from military practice. See G.N.A.S. Rules.

COACHING CERTIFICATES   Instructor/County Coach/Regional Coach/National Coach.

COCK FEATHER   The fletching at right-angles to the nock.

COMPOSITE BOW   A bow which has a number of materials glued together to form the limbs.

CREEPING   Failure to maintain draw length while on hold.

CRESTING   The coloured bands on the shaft of an arrow to aid identification.

CROSS-BOW   A bow with a mechanical lock and trigger.

DACRON   Polyester string material.

D.F.L.   The draw-force line. It should be a straight line between the point of pressure on the bow handle, the nock of the arrow, and the point of the drawing elbow at full draw.

DEAD LOOSE   A loose in which only the fingers move to release the string.

DOMINANT EYE   The eye preferred by the archer for the purposes of aiming, even when both eyes are open.

DRAW   The act of extending the bow and string.

DRAW-CHECK   A device to tell the archer when the draw is complete.

DRAW-LENGTH   (1)   The distance to which a bow is designed to be drawn.

(2)   The distance to which an archer is capable of drawing efficiently.

DRAW-WEIGHT   The effort required to draw a bow a stated distance.

E.F.A.A.   English Field Archery Association.

END   Three or six arrows shot before collection.

E.S.A.R.   The eye, sight, arrow relationship. It should be in a true vertical plane.

FAST!   The warning cry: 'Hold fast to the string, and come down!'

FIBRE-GLASS   Material combined with plastic used to make practice bows and to make laminations for composite bows.

FIELD CAPTAIN   The officer in charge of shooting at a meeting.

FIELD SHOOTING   A form of archery at a wide variety of ranges in rough country. See G.N.A.S. Rules, and E.F.A.A. Rules.

FINGER TAB   A shield worn on the loosing fingers to ensure consistency of loose.

FISTMELE   The distance measured by an archer's palm and extended thumb, used as a rough guide to bracing-height.

F.I.T.A.   Fédération Internationale de Tir à l'Arc. The International governing body for Archery.

FLETCH   To fit feather or plastic vanes to an arrow shaft.

FLETCHINGS   The feathers or vanes on the arrow.

FLETCHING JIG   A device to hold fletchings in position while being glued.

FLIGHT SHOOTING   Shooting for the longest possible distance. See G.N.A.S. Rules.

FOLLOW-THROUGH   The continued parting of the hands after loosing without deviation.

FOOTMARKERS   Small discs, of specified height, used to mark an archer's standing position.

FORWARD LOOSE   Loose in which the hand moves forward before the string is released.

FREESTYLE   Form of Field Shooting in which sights are permitted.

G.N.A.S.   Grand National Archery Society. The governing body of Archery throughout the United Kingdom.

GOLD   The central yellow zone of the target (or the 10-zone of an international face).

GRAND MASTER BOWMAN   Archer who has demonstrated superlative shooting ability at the highest level.

GROUND QUIVER   A holder for arrows and bow, stuck into the ground.

GROUPING   Getting one's arrows close together in the target.

HANDICAP NUMBER   The code by which an archer is graded according to ability.

HANDLE   The part of the bow held in the hand.

HANGER   An arrow that hangs loose in the target.

HEELING   Applying pressure on the bow-handle below the point of balance (or rather, below the tiller-point).

HOLDING   Maintaining the aim and draw-length before loosing.

HUNTING   Shooting in the bow at live game.

I.F.A.A.   International Field Archery Association.

KEVLAR   Carbon-fibre string material.

KISSER   A disc on the string, of specified maximum size, to indicate to the archer the point on the string which is drawn to the lips.

LADY PARAMOUNT   Originally the patroness of an archery meeting; nowadays the lady invited to present the prizes.

LIMB   Either part of the bow above or below the handle section.

LOADED BOW   A bow with an arrow on the string.

LONG BOW   A bow of English (or rather, Welsh) traditional design.

LOOSE   The act of releasing the string.

MARK   The object which the archer intends to hit.

MASTER BOWMAN   An archer who has reached certain prescribed high scores in target archery at major tournaments.

MASTER BOWMAN (FIELD)   As above, in Field Archery.

NOCK (of arrow)   The slot at the end of the arrow that fits onto the string.

NOCK (of bow)   Slots in the ends of the bow limbs in which the string is retained.

NOCKING POINT   The precise point on the string where the nock of the arrow should be located.

OVERBOWED   Provided with a bow too strong to manage efficiently.

OVERBRACED   Of a bow, being braced higher than intended by the bowyer.

OVERDRAWING   (1)   Drawing the string further than the bowyer intended.

(2)   Drawing the arrow clear past the arrow pass.

PILE   The simple pointed end of a target arrow.

PINCHING   Nipping the nock tightly between the fingers.

PINHOLE   The dead centre of the target.

POINT OF AIM   Aiming by means of referring the pile to some aiming-point, not necessarily the target itself.

POKER   Rod projecting from the bow as a form of stabiliser.

POPINJAY SHOOTING   Shooting at artificial birds arranged on a perch at the top of a mast. See G.N.A.S. Rules.

POST   Station in Field Archery from which a shot, or shots, are taken.

PRACTICE BOW   A bow of light draw-weight used for teaching beginners.

PREP. LINE   The desirably straight line before drawing, of forearm and shaft.

QUIVER   A holder for arrows while shooting is in progress.

ROUND   A given number of arrows shot under stated conditions.

ROVING   Shooting at chance marks in open country.

SERVING   The whipping on the string to check fraying by the fingers.

SERVING TOOL   A device to lay the whipping on regularly under even tension.

SHAFT   The arrow cylinder itself.

SHAFT ARM   The arm that draws the string.

SHAFT FEATHERS   The fletchings that lie nearest to the bow.

SHOOTING LINE   The line across which the archer stands.

SHOULDER QUIVER   Arrow holder worn on the back, particularly by Field Archers.

SIGHTERS   Unscored arrows shot before a round so that sights, etc., may be adjusted.

SKIRT   The part of the target outside the scoring zones.

SLING   A device to enable the bow to be shot without being held.

SNAP-SHOOTING   Loosing without pause on aim.

SPECTATORS' LINE   Line at least 15 yards behind the shooting line.

SPINE   The measure of the bending factor of an arrow.

SPINE-RATING   As above, expressed in terms of one-hundredths of an inch deflection when a $1\frac{1}{2}$ lb. weight is hung on the centre of the arrow.

SPOT   (1)   The central scoring zone of a Field Target.

(2)   To observe the fall of individual arrows in Field Archery.

STABILISERS   Weights attached to the bow to reduce tendency to move it away from the mark or to reduce torque.

STACKING   An extreme increase in draw-weight of a bow as it approaches its draw-length.

STRING   "Endless"   One in which the constituent strands are brought together by whipping to form loops.

"Laid in" One in which the loops are formed by splicing or by twisting in a special fashion.

TAB Same as for finger tab.

TACKLE The archer's shooting equipment.

TARGET CAPTAIN He who is appointed to be in charge of the archers on his target. He is also responsible for scoring.

TARGET DAY Day officially set aside by a club for formal shooting.

TARGET FACE Material cover for target boss on which scoring zones are painted or printed.

TARGET LIEUTENANT Assistant to the Target Captain.

TARGET STAND Wooden stand supporting the boss.

TILLER To correct the curvature of a bow by using a tiller (or notched bar to hold bow drawn at a variety of draw-lengths).

TILLER-POINT Point on the handle of the bow from which the limbs have been constructed to bend symmetrically.

TIMBER HITCH A kind of knot (or rather, bend) used to secure the lower end of a single-loop bowstring.

TORQUE Turning-force applied to the bow in either a horizontal or vertical direction.

UNDERBOWED Using a weaker bow than desirable.

UNDERDRAWN Insufficient arrow length drawn in the bow.

UNIT-AIMING Adjusting for aim at the waist, preserving the line of arms and shoulders.

WAITING LINE Line behind which archers retire after shooting, at least 5 yards behind the shooting line.

WEIGHT-IN-HAND The actual physical weight of the bow, not its power.

YEW Wood used for the best traditional English long bows.

ZEN Japanese religious ritual, including practice of archery as an art-form.

INDEX

A.A.S. (Association for Archery in Schools), 118, 121
aiming, 38, 39, 42, 88
alloy tubing, 20
arrow length, 21, 26
arrows, 19, 62, 93, 128

Barebow, 43, 45, 85, 146
'Basic' method of instruction, 31, 43, 77, 117, 146
binoculars, 73
blind loosing, 87
blunts, 110
boss, 133, 146
bows, 17, 26, 34, 54, 55, 124
bow window, 84, 86
brace, 32
bracer, 22, 26, 132, 146
bracing-height, 77, 92, 146
butt, 135

calibration, 44
cant, 84
cast, 59
C.C.P.R. (Central Council of Physical Recreation), 15
Certificate of Competence, 117
clicker, 87, 147
clocking, 93, 147
clout, 49–54, 106, 147
clubs, 15, 139
cock feathers, 21, 35, 129, 147
composite bow, 59
controlling eye, 31
creeping, 84, 87, 147
cut-out, 59

Dacron, 125
darts, 111, 146
D.F.L. (Draw Force Line), 80, 88, 147

dog-legging, 84
dominant eye, 31, 147
draw-weight, 56, 147

E.S.A.R. (the eye, sight, arrow relationship), 83, 85, 147

faces, 102, 135
fast, 27, 147
Field Archery, 28, 43, 101–104, 148
F.I.T.A. (Fédération Internationale de Tir à l'Arc), 141, 147
fletching, 20, 68, 129, 148
Flight shooting, 104, 148
follow-through, 41, 88, 148
Freestyle, 43, 148
full draw, 36, 38

G.N.A.S. (Grand National Archery Society), 15, 16, 140, 141, 148
golf, 110
ground quiver, 16, 24, 148
group, 78, 148

hand hold on bow, 88
handicap, 101, 121, 148
head position, 34
heeling, 80
horizontal errors, 83
hunting, 101, 149

instinctive archery, 43, 48

Kevlar, 125, 149
kisser, 52, 149

leader board, 12
loose, 36, 39, 147, 149
loosing, 39, 86

153

nock, 67, 130, 149
nocking, 34
nocking point, 19

overshot, 28

paradox, archer's, 64, 146
paraplegics, 13, 114
piles, 66, 130
plastic vanes, 21
polaroid camera, 95
pony crupp butt, 23
popinjay, 108, 150
prep. line (preparation position), 35,
    150

quiver, 71, 132

relaxation, 90, 92
rounds, 100, 121, 122, 150

scratcher, 73
sight, 39, 44, 59, 146
space picture, 45
spine, 20, 63, 150
squad, 95
stabilisers, 58, 150
standing position, 33, 44
stands, 135, 137
string, 62, 94, 125–8

tabs, 23, 132, 148
team manager, 96
tension, 89
tiller, 23, 132, 151
torque, 84, 151
Toxophilus, 76

unit aiming, 88, 15

vertical errors, 79

whistle code, 27